Global
Organizations

Richard Pettinger

- Fast track route to understanding the organizational, economic and managerial pressures and constraints in global enterprises

- Covers the key areas of strategic, marketing and financial priorities and demands and the need for corporate social, cultural and operational awareness and responsibility

- Examples and lessons from some of the world's most successful businesses, including ABB, Nissan and Mattel Inc, and ideas from the world's smartest thinkers, including Gary Hamel, Peter Drucker, Naomi Klein, Sumantra Ghoshal and Chris Bartlett

- Includes a glossary of key concepts and a comprehensive resources guide

>>EXPRESS EXEC.COM<<
essential management thinking at your fingertips

The right of Richard Pettinger to be identified as the author of this work has been asserted in accordance with the Copyright, Designs and Patents Act 1988

First published 2002 by
Capstone Publishing (a Wiley company)
8 Newtec Place
Magdalen Road
Oxford OX4 1RE
United Kingdom
http://www.capstoneideas.com

CIP catalogue records for this book are available from the British Library and the US Library of Congress

ISBN 1-84112-237-8

Printed and bound by CPI Antony Rowe, Eastbourne

This book is printed on acid-free paper

Substantial discounts on bulk quantities of Capstone books are available to corporations, professional associations and other organizations. Please contact Capstone for more details on +44 (0)1865 798 623 or (fax) +44 (0)1865 240 941 or (e-mail) info@wiley-capstone.co.uk

Contents

Introduction to ExpressExec

ExpressExec is 3 million words of the latest management thinking compiled into 10 modules. Each module contains 10 individual titles forming a comprehensive resource of current business practice written by leading practitioners in their field. From brand management to balanced scorecard, ExpressExec enables you to grasp the key concepts behind each subject and implement the theory immediately. Each of the 100 titles is available in print and electronic formats.

Through the ExpressExec.com Website you will discover that you can access the complete resource in a number of ways:

» printed books or e-books;
» e-content – PDF or XML (for licensed syndication) adding value to an intranet or Internet site;
» a corporate e-learning/knowledge management solution providing a cost-effective platform for developing skills and sharing knowledge within an organization;
» bespoke delivery – tailored solutions to solve your need.

Why not visit www.expressexec.com and register for free key management briefings, a monthly newsletter and interactive skills checklists. Share your ideas about ExpressExec and your thoughts about business today.

Please contact elound@wiley-capstone.co.uk for more information.

Introduction to Global Organizations

This chapter considers multinational companies and corporate and collective responsibility.

There is a revolution in business and public services presently going on in every corner of the world. It is being led by global organizations and their managers, and driven by the financial and technological power and influence that they wield. However localized activities were in the past, the potential for competition exists, and is increasing, in all sectors.

BACKGROUND

The background against which this revolution is taking place is one of economic, social and political turbulence. In the recent past there have been stock market and currency crashes, wars, revolutions and economic recessions in many parts of the world. The industrial and post-industrial economies of the West are undergoing radical transformation, driven by technological advance and the emergence of competition from Asia, Central and South America, and the newly independent states of the former USSR. The Japanese have generated an industrial and commercial power block that dominates the global, electrical and consumer goods markets and makes them major operators in the automobile, white goods and finance sectors.

MULTINATIONAL COMPANIES

The revolution is being driven by global organizations and multinational companies (MNCs). These companies are able, by virtue of their size and command of resources, technology, expertise and finance, to engage in all kinds of activity anywhere in the world where they see an opportunity. This is exactly at the time when a rapidly increasing global population is placing ever-greater strains on finite and diminishing natural resources. These have to be planned, ordered and organized to ensure that they are used to the greatest possible advantage.

Because of their size and ability to locate anywhere in the world, the process by which the revolution is being driven is led also by global organizations and MNCs. These organizations, and their managers, are able to set and establish price, quality, value and volume levels of products and services. They determine the basis on which each is offered for sale and consumption. They determine the locations, where each product or service is offered, and the trading conditions attached. They exert influence in political and macro-economic circles, both with individual governments, and also trans-governmental bodies such as the United Nations (UN), World Trade Organization (WTO), World Bank (WB) and the North Atlantic Treaty Organization (NATO).

CORPORATE AND COLLECTIVE RESPONSIBILITY

Many would argue that organizations able to operate in these ways have specific responsibilities for:

» absolute standards of product and service quality;
» the quality of working life of all those working either directly for them, or else as subcontractors; and
» economic, political and social stability in specific locations where they have influence. This especially applies to those locating manufacturing operations in under-developed countries where Western and Japanese MNCs are able, if they so choose, to dictate patterns and volumes of employment, wage levels and other terms and conditions (see summary box 1.1).

SUMMARY BOX 1.1: GLOBAL CAPITALISM

The nature, level, and influence of multinational activities have caused widespread economic, social and political concern, and this has been extensively reported in the media.

These concerns have led to demonstrations and the creation of protest movements in many Western cities against the ways in which both governments and global organizations are known, believed, and perceived to be exerting influence on the consumer habits and lifestyles of the West, and employment patterns and conditions in the third world. The protests have been directed at:

» government and political actions perceived to be endorsing the influence of global organizations and MNCs; in particular the perceived lack of government capability and willingness to do anything about excesses of labor and resource exploitation;

» the known, believed and perceived lack of integrity of the activities of MNCs in sourcing supplies and products;
» the known, believed and perceived domination of consumer markets. This is supported by the fact and perception of global organizations' ability to dominate consumer outlets and to squeeze others out;
» profit levels achieved, compounded by the fact and perception that profits are then retained by stockholders rather than being reinvested in the emerging economies; and
» third world debt problems. This requires many countries to accept investment from global organizations and MNCs on conditions imposed and as a consequence of political support, rather than according to the needs of the particular country.

This level of economic, social, and political power and influence brings clear responsibilities and obligations. In many cases, it is being recognized by much of the Western public at large that there are shortfalls in corporate integrity.

CONCLUSIONS

Because of their sheer size and ability to operate anywhere, global organizations and MNCs exert great influence. They carry responsibilities based on integrity and economic and social justice, in addition to their own long-term profitability. These strands indicate the two elements necessary for the productive and responsible development of markets, operations, activities, and the society in the areas where global organizations have influence. Managers of global organizations must, at present, be concerned with economic development; the more responsible and enlightened also take their social and political responsibilities seriously. For long-term sustained (and sustainable) growth and development both strands are equally important.

What are Global Organizations?

Most people can name a global organization, but their range is harder to define. This chapter examines various aspects of global organizations, including global presence, influence and domination of the developed world.

INTRODUCTION

The United Nations has 217 member states; and to be truly global, organizations would need to have a presence in each of them. However,
global organizations and MNCs come in many forms. A global organization is recognized as such if it has a presence or influence in many
countries. An MNC must have a presence in two or more countries. It
is therefore useful to distinguish between different forms of powerful
and influential organizations as follows.

GLOBAL PRESENCE

There are very few organizations that have a presence in most, or all,
countries of the world. Coca-Cola is one, though its products are still not
available to about half the world's population. Microsoft has a presence
reaching into government and trans-governmental organizations such
as the UN and NATO. It also has business headquarters in all countries
(including Albania and North Korea); but again, does not yet reach
about half the population of the world. ABB, the engineering group of
companies, has carried out project work in every country, often in joint
ventures and with local partners. The products of SmithKlineGlaxo,
the pharmaceuticals giant, are available in most countries of the world
(whether manufactured directly or made under license).

GLOBAL INFLUENCE

Organizations with global influence set the standards of product quality
and service delivery in developed markets, and can impose these
elsewhere.

Some organizations produce goods and services to different standards
according to the nature, location and demands of markets. Others
produce to more or less universal standards and vary the price by
location (e.g. car manufacturers). Others produce differentiated goods
and services offered under different names according to sector or
location (e.g. Volkswagen and its use of the Seat and Skoda brands).

GLOBAL OLIGOPOLIES

Because of the dominance of the particular world markets by a few large
organizations, those involved set global standards and price, quality,

value, and volume mixes, even though each individual company may not itself have a truly global presence. This applies especially to airliner manufacture where the market is more or less equally divided between Boeing and Airbus; information technology systems, where everything has to be compatible with Microsoft and IBM; and oil and petrol supply dominated by Esso, BP, Texaco, Elf, Shell and Aramco.

GLOBAL ACCESS

Organizations that *can* go anywhere in the world include each of the above. This also applies to those whose products and services are in demand. This may be because they are known, believed or perceived to be of high quality and value. It may be because they are perceived to be in high demand (e.g. McDonald's has a presence in 130 countries).

More insidiously, it may be because emerging nations have been told to use particular organizations, products and services as a condition of finance from the West. For example, KPMG, the UK management consultancy, has a presence in 156 countries and McKinsey and Co., the American management consultancy, in 133 countries. Both work extensively in government (see summary box 2.1).

SUMMARY BOX 2.1: POLISH STATE RAILWAYS

After the fall of the USSR, Poland sought to establish a political, economic and social infrastructure aimed at early membership of the EU.

The EU required conditions. Above all, these referred to the restructuring of energy, telecommunications and transport infrastructure. The state airline, LOT, joined the One World Alliance, and became a joint partner with British Airways on some routes.

Polish State Railways remained the main arm of internal public transport. During the communist period, it was operated as a state monopoly under one bureaucracy. The EU required it to become "leaner and fitter." UK consultants were appointed. The company was privatized and broken up into individual organizations responsible for: track infrastructure, signaling, maintenance, national passenger services, regional passenger services, national freight services, local freight services, and international services. Polish State Railways also incorporated a travel agency, travel and ticketing services, locomotive, carriage and wagon construction and maintenance. Some of this was conducted locally; most required the involvement of an EU partner (e.g. ABB were the prescribed contractor for locomotive manufacturing and maintenance).

The EU required most aspects to be conducted with French, German, Italian, Swedish and UK partners to establish "the necessary standards." Accordingly, the restructuring produced a railway system modeled along the lines previously adopted in the UK.

At the beginning of the twenty-first century, both the UK and the Polish railway industries reported "strategic and operational difficulties."

Organizations that *can* go anywhere in the world include Red Cross, the Catholic Church and other religious foundations, Medecins sans Frontieres, Oxfam, and organs of the UN including UNICEF (the United Nations Children's Foundation), and UNHCR (the United Nations High Commission on Refugees). These organizations have specific constitutions, agenda, and remits. They also carry extensive primary and derived responsibilities.

However, in pursuit of the primary purpose of carrying out missionary work or feeding the hungry these organizations' presences in various countries have from time to time been unwelcome or compromised (see summary box 2.2).

SUMMARY BOX 2.2: RESPONSIBILITY AND COMPROMISE AT OXFAM

In order to be able to get supplies into war zones and remote locations, Oxfam, the relief aid charity, has, from time to time, been forced to carry arms shipments on its relief planes. The organization has to pay bribes in some states and locations. It has, at times, accepted donations from commercial global organizations and MNCs on the condition that the brand name is prominently displayed. Most notoriously of all, the organization was once drawn into the marketing and distribution of "infant formula," a high calorie branded substitute for breast milk produced by Nestle that was to be fed to newborn babies. Because of the high cost, those working in remote parts of Africa and the Far East over-diluted the product, accelerating, rather than alleviating, malnutrition.

Oxfam staff had to work alongside nurses and other medical personnel wearing branded uniforms. These staff were given unlimited access to maternity wards in local hospitals, and this eventually led to a serious conflict between Oxfam (and other relief charities and agencies) and the supplying company.

Organizations that *can* go anywhere include news and media companies. Many of these are themselves global in terms of their reach and access (e.g. BBC, CNN, NewsCorp). Others, though more or less parochial, exert a derived global influence (e.g. the Financial Times and Wall Street Journal whose reportage of EU, US and Japanese MNCs affects the majority of investment decisions in some way).

The responsibility here is the reporting of events, rather than setting the news agenda and diverting attention to those stories that attract advertising and sponsorship revenues, and away from those issues that are deemed either:

» not in the public interest – itself a phrase with heavy responsibility; or

» not in the political or other vested interest – in which governments and commercial interests are able to influence journalists and broadcasters either to leave a story altogether, or else give it a distinctive favorable slant (see summary box 2.3).

SUMMARY BOX 2.3: "TRUTH IS THE FIRST CASUALTY OF WAR." (W.S. CHURCHILL)

In the summer of 1999, the news agenda was set for over a week by CNN. The company happened to be filming a documentary in a

Palestinian refugee camp when it was shelled by the Israelis. Also in 1999, representatives of Oxfam, Red Cross and Medecins sans Frontieres each went on global television to announce that there would be a humanitarian disaster in the refugee camps of Rwanda unless substantial aid was poured in. Millions, they forecast, would die. In the event, 196 died, one a newborn baby, the others as the result of internal gang warfare within the camps.

DOMINATION OF THE DEVELOPED WORLD

Organizations that dominate the developed world are sometimes referred to as "axis global organizations." These have an overwhelming influence and presence in the "commercial axis" of the USA, EU and Japan. These organizations set price, quality, value and volume levels of capital and consumer goods and services, and standards of overall organizational performance. They establish levels of investment; staff rewards, terms and conditions of employment; quality of working life and labor relations; and strategic and operations management. They set standards for environment management and quality of social life.

They step out of the "axis" at any point in their chain of operations, where they believe it is in their interests to do so. The most common areas include the following:

» *Supply side* – in which supplies are sought from areas where they are most prolific and readily available; or where the relationship can be dominated by the axis organization.

» *Manufacturing* – in which axis organizations locate or subcontract their manufacturing processes at places most suitable to serve their markets (e.g. Toyota and Sony in Poland); or where labor is cheap (e.g. branded, garment and sportswear manufacture in Malaysia, Thailand, Pakistan and Cambodia).

» *Distribution* – in which axis companies place their distribution operations under flags of convenience allowing them to employ staff on expedient/favorable terms and conditions of employment, and to operate to minimum standards of safety and security. This is standard practice in sea transport, and becoming more widespread in air and road activities.

» *Effluent disposal* – in which organizations are able to pay Third World governments to relieve them of waste and effluent for a fraction of the cost of disposing of it properly, and in an environmentally friendly manner, or of reprocessing it themselves.

OTHER GLOBAL INFLUENCE

These are organizations that exert global influence of some sort whether or not they have a physical global presence. For example:

» global icons such as Walt Disney, setting standards for film production and delivery;
» standards of consumer goods manufacturing, quality, and durability have long since been set by Japanese companies;
» global mobile telephone production is dominated by Nokia and Ericcsson (Finland);
» fashion design is dominated by exhibitions and trade fairs in London, Paris, Milan, and New York;
» hotel facility standards, which were originally set by Hilton and subsequently adopted by all those who sought a sustainable competitive position and commercial advantages in the sector; and
» individualized corporations, whereby expansion and globalization are based on the individual and collective talents of those involved (see below, Chapter 9).

Also, any organization that sets or transforms any part of practice or activities has global influence. This may be extended to organization and managerial principles and practice (e.g. Semco); advertising (J. Walter Thompson); management consultancy (McKinsey); Website development and commercialization (Amazon).

CONCLUSIONS

The prerequisites for being a global organization are:

» size, scope and scale of resources to enable activities to be established anywhere in the world; and
» recognition of the full range of collective and individual responsibilities that this capability brings.

To this should be added:

» the capability to think globally;
» the capability and willingness to develop a global set of values; and
» the capability and willingness to understand, and be comfortable with, the demands and expectations of any part of the world in which business is sought.

None of this is to be confused with the belief or perception that a particular domestic format *can* be imposed on different parts of the world through sheer economic force. While it is true that, in many cases, this continues to be achieved, long-term globalization comes with the full range of responsibilities and obligations indicated, as well as the economic might.

KEY LEARNING POINTS

Global organizations:

» are characterized by power and influence;
» have absolute and actual attitudes to responsibility;
» achieve a global presence in different ways;
» have a position of economic strength, but also attendant responsibilities; and
» have different attitudes to globalization and have varying worldwide influences.

Evolution of Global Organizations

The modern idea of global organizations is based on patterns of military conquest and trade. This chapter examines how the concept of global organizations has evolved.

INTRODUCTION

The history of global organizations is based on patterns of military conquest and trade. These are relatively well documented in Europe, parts of the Middle East, and Asia; less so in North and South America, and Africa. The earliest "global organizations" were the armies of the then *known* world: the Persians under Alexander the Great, the Assyrians of Nebuchadnezzar, the Carthaginians under Hannibal, and then the Romans.

MILITARY CONQUEST

The Roman conquests and history and development of the empire that resulted bring some fundamental lessons for all organizations that seek to become global. These include the following.

» The need for local acceptance. In those parts of the empire where there were wars and rebellions, this was as the result of bad, inappropriate or unsympathetic local leadership and direction, overwhelming demands from the center (Rome), or oppressive approaches to the local people.
» The need to draw the best from the center and the particular locality so that everyone benefited (this lesson was subsequently applied with great effect by the Japanese manufacturing companies as they established in the West in the 1970s and beyond).
» Managing the local workforces effectively. The Romans imposed their own provincial governors and officer corps. Much of the rest of the work required had to be carried out by the local population. This meant employing the population as administrators, builders, and soldiers, for which full Roman citizenship was the reward.

The empire finally fell when the barbarian (non-Roman) regiments of the army rebelled under the general Theodosius; and he then led a march on Rome itself, which was destroyed. Theodosius himself was installed as the first non-Roman emperor in 486 AD (see summary box 3.1).

SUMMARY BOX 3.1: THE LEGACY OF CONSTANTINE

Constantine is universally known as the Roman emperor who brought Christianity to the empire in 322 AD. An act of faith and belief it may have been. It certainly had a major managerial spin-off. Each of the big cities of the empire had Christian communities; and these tended to be better educated than the rest of the population. Accordingly, Constantine found himself with supporters in every area who were capable, educated and aware, as well as having a distinctive set of values. He could trust them; and they trusted him.

THE FOUNDATIONS OF EUROPEAN EMPIRES

In 1492, Christopher Columbus set sail from Cadiz, Spain to discover the western sea route to India. The overland route out of Eastern Europe was by then well known, having been opened up centuries earlier by Marco Polo in travels to China and India.

The voyages of Columbus, and others who followed him, found rich and fertile lands and civilizations, and the European nation states claimed them as their own. Various forms of leadership and management were imposed on the new empires including:

» Military – imposed by Spain and Portugal on Central and South America and subsequently reinforced by the Catholic Church and the Inquisition, as the native population was required to conform to the norms, values, and religion of the conquerors.
» Ad hoc – favored by the English in which appointments were granted to individuals on the basis of what they would bring home from the new world. The English established permanent colonies very much later. The first were in what is now the "New England" part of northeastern USA. Fleeing religious persecution in England, those who arrived in the new world established collective and participative communities, and sought both friendly trading relations with the native population, and also to convert them to Christianity.

» Direct rule from Europe – imposed by the French on their colonies in the West Indies and Canada. This worked so long as there was peaceful coexistence. It eventually had to be abandoned because of increases in piracy in the West Indies and military campaigning by the English in Canada.

The foundation periods and activities in the fledgling European empires reinforced the need for coexistence and mutual interest. In many cases, these lessons were not properly learned. This in turn, however, reinforced the *need for attention to logistics, transport management, and investment*. Activities in the fledgling European empires reinforced the need for coexistence and mutual interest. It was also essential to recognize the *need for effective logistics, transport management, and investment*, especially ordering and managing activities physically remote from the center of power and authority.

There is also a lesson for the future, not yet realized, that colonies ultimately want their own independence and autonomy.

THE BEGINNINGS OF CORPORATISM

Alongside the political and military developments came the first overseas trading companies. Both the Dutch and English had East India companies. The English established the London and Rhodesia Company (Lonrho), the South Sea Islands Company, and the Ceylon Tea Company among others to conduct trade between the home country and the named part of the world, alongside the political and military expansion.

The period also marked the beginnings of stock markets. At first, people bought shares to finance a particular voyage or venture and they would receive a reward (dividend) when the goods were brought home and sold on. The practice then developed into company financing so that people would share in the total performance and profitability of the company (see summary box 3.2).

SUMMARY BOX 3.2: SOUTH SEA ISLAND COMPANY

In the mid eighteenth century, the South Sea Island Company created the first share scandal. Promising high dividend levels to all those who invested, a "bubble" was created in which the shares themselves became a commodity. There was a buying frenzy. Those who could afford them bought shares. Those who could not took out bank loans or clubbed together. The result was a steep increase in the price of the shares – in spite of the fact that the only returns available were the ability to sell the share on again, or dividends payable when the cargoes returned. When the cargoes returned they were worthless. The bubble burst. Everyone who held the shares lost their money. There were riots in London directed at the company owners and the banks which had lent the money.

In spite of setbacks, the practice developed to the point at which neither ventures nor companies ever needed to be dependent solely on political, royal or wealthy patronage. The practice was also developed so that liability was limited to the face value of the share rather than its sale price. By keeping face values low, much broader interests and resources were drawn in. The practice institutionalized the following.

» The advent of shares, and therefore companies, as commodities in their own right.
» The principle of profit returns and dividends.
» The conduct of trade by companies independent of government or political direction.
» The ability to trade anywhere in the world provided that a mutually advantageous basis could be established.
» The ability to locate away from the country of origin.
» The fledgling ability to dominate particular markets and activities (see summary box 3.3).

SUMMARY BOX 3.3: THE BOSTON TEA COMPANY

The Boston Tea Company was based in Bristol, UK. In the late eighteenth century it carried cargoes of tea to New England, returning with Virginia tobacco and cotton. In the latter half of the century it became identified by the indigenous population as a symbol of colonial exploitation. Matters came to a head when it refused to renegotiate carriage terms for the tobacco growers. There were also accusations of profiteering in the prices it charged for tea and its ability to limit supplies, as it was the monopoly carrier. On Christmas Day 1775, the company's ships were stormed by a mob in Boston, Massachusetts, and they threw the cargo of tea into the harbor. This came to be known as "the Boston tea party."

The Boston tea party was an early example of an organized anti-capitalist demonstration. It has also come to be recognized as the first action of the American War of Independence.

THE CONTROL OF PARTICULAR INDUSTRIES

Shipping

Global trade became universally possible with the development of shipping fleets, first sailing and then steam-powered vessels. The first globally influential organizations were therefore the shipping lines. They decided who, and what, could be carried, when, where, and for how much. They were responsible for rapid growth in indigenous shipbuilding and, by extrapolation, expansion of the iron, steel, and coal industries.

The companies operated independently rather than combining into conglomerates. Each had its own route network with the home port as the starting point. Some routes were extremely profitable and attracted competition. Accordingly, companies began to seek advantages through being the fastest or most reliable, or through carrying both passengers and freight (see summary box 3.4).

SUMMARY BOX 3.4: EARLY COMPETITION

Ships bringing tea and spices to Europe from the Far East would find themselves racing each other back to the home port because there were price advantages for the first cargoes home. The ships that served the Wills tobacco family enhanced their collective return on investment by operating a "golden triangle route." Leaving Bristol, the company delivered arms and supplies to the garrisons of the British colonies of West Africa. From there, the company carried cargoes of slaves to the plantations of North America and returned with tobacco and cotton. The ships therefore, always traveled full. By the beginning of the twentieth century shipping networks covered the globe. Each European country had its own route network, national companies, and trading partners. The USA also began to develop its own shipping fleet.

Arms races

Shipping and transport technology developed further as the result of nineteenth century European imperialism and the need both to be able to attack and defend when required. National shipping fleets were consequently developed to include warships and troop ships; and commercial lines were to have their ships commandeered for war efforts. Ships therefore had to be fast, reliable and capable of extended stays at sea; they also had to be effective fighting and defensive machines.

Warship development greatly enhanced the prestige and value of shipyards and related industries. This also marked the beginning of the broader value of the supply side. High quality gunnery and ordnance from Bofors, Nobel and Mond (all Swedish) were bought for armies and navies in the UK, France and Germany. Local competing industries were subsequently developed.

Military advances and the creation of empires by the Europeans opened up fresh trade routes, as well as developing shipping and warfare technology. Empires created their own markets and opportunities, and the global principles of technology, market, and relationship development first became established.

Arms races continued throughout the developed world for the duration of the twentieth century. These were fuelled by World War I (1914-1918), World War II (1939-1945), and, subsequently, the Cold War (1947-1990). The companies involved in the armaments industry came, by virtue of their technological expertise, to be able to make substantial contributions to commercial markets.

Mass production

The invention of the production line transformed the uniformity, availability and reliability of goods and services. The most famous early commercial production line was built by Ford at Detroit in the first part of the twentieth century. Based on the "principles of scientific management" of F.W. Taylor (see Chapter 8) every task was rigorously controlled to ensure complete standardization.

Economies of scale were achieved and this meant that a greater volume of products could be made available at decreasing prices. This accelerated the development of domestic markets and made products available for export. It also caused manufacturing companies to think of where else they could locate in order to open up fresh markets (see summary box 3.5).

SUMMARY BOX 3.5: FORD

After World War I, Ford established factories in the UK, Spain, and Germany. The company produced cars and trucks, as well as its own components.

In November 1998, as reported by *The Times*, documents came to light indicating that the company's German operations had continued producing trucks and other transport for the Wehrmacht throughout World War II. The company had also used forced labor imported from countries conquered by the Germans.

This is an early example of companies operating across borders and in spite of the prevailing political situation.

Mass production transformed

There are two clear stages in the transformation of mass production. The first was in World War II, whereby everything in all the warring countries was put on to this form of approach. For example, by the end of 1942, the Russians were producing 300 tanks, 180 railway wagons and 900 guns per day; in the US Boeing produced 100 B25 super-bombers per week; German shipyards produced one submarine every nine days. The lessons learned would then be applied to the post-war rebuilding of all the nations, subject only to investment and resources being made available.

The second transformation came from the late 1960s onwards and was led by the Japanese. European and North American mass production concentrated on volume. The result was a great proliferation of mass market goods – all homes could now have a car, refrigerator, television, hi-fi, electrical kettles; foodstuffs were tinned, dried, packaged, and frozen. Prices came tumbling down.

The quality was variable, especially the reliability of cars, white goods, and other electrical products. The Japanese brought quality and reliability to mass production. Supported by high levels of investment, and often underwritten by the Japanese government central bank, unit production costs fell to the point at which the combination of price advantage, enhanced quality and reliability, and the perceived permanence of the companies themselves, made the products irresistible.

The key feature of the Japanese ethos was (and remains) *Kaizen* – the quest for continuous improvement. Mass production was no longer therefore an end in itself; anything that was made could be developed further. The companies had cost and price advantages that could be exploited. This led to accusations of market flooding and product dumping. However, in most cases, the Japanese product was at least as expensive as the European or North American equivalent. Customers chose to pay for the enhanced quality and perceived benefits (and this was in spite of deeply held prejudices against the Japanese, the legacy of the brutality of World War II in the Far East). The fact that the producer was not indigenous was ultimately of no consequence. Customers demanded satisfaction, and Japanese producers provided it.

LOCATION

Over the last part of the twentieth century Japanese companies established manufacturing activities in other parts of the developed world. They brought the following.

» *The Keiretsu organization* – retaining as much as possible in-house and therefore capable of overall control.
» *A long-term view* – factories and outlets were established on the basis that they would be there for a long time (in contrast for example,

to subcontracting arrangements in the garment and foodstuffs industries where companies switched suppliers at very short notice). The aim is to develop corporate citizens, as well as employment providers.

» *Distinctive staffing policies* – based on security of employment, fully flexible working practices, multi-skilling – and high levels of wages in return for high value work. The companies engage in partnership and consultation arrangements with staff representatives and recognized trade unions. The attitude is positive and cooperative. Companies take the view that positive labor relations contribute to profits; and that negative, adversarial and confrontational approaches are divisive and disruptive, requiring additional expenditure on HR, labor relations specialists and problem-solvers. Procedures are streamlined and simple to operate.

» *Lifetime employment* – based on full multi-skilling and continuous development, allowing staff to shift from one area of activity to others if schedules demand; and allowing the company to change products if required (e.g. Mitsubishi changed from ships and airplanes to cars in the 1970s without a single job loss). In practice, this has not been possible to sustain in all areas, though compulsory lay-offs have been very few, especially compared to Western companies.

» *Continued high levels of investment* – in production technology and the capability of staff to use it to maximum advantage. Companies take the view that no technology is valuable unless staff can use it (see summary box 3.6).

SUMMARY BOX 3.6: THE INVESTMENT PARABLE

The tale is told of two groups of managers, one from the West and one Japanese, who each ran a production line employing 20 people. A machine was invented that could do the work of this line but which only required one person to operate it. The Western managers went home with heavy hearts because they knew they would have to compulsorily lay-off 19 people. The Japanese managers went home with glad hearts because they were going to get 20 new machines; they were going to expand output by a factor of 20; all the staff were going to get retraining and a fresh place of work; and they would not be adding to the wage bill.

» *Market development* in which the approach has been to combine high brand awareness with absolute standards of quality and performance so that:
  » perceived consumer confidence continues to be assured;
  » consumers will continue to be favorably disposed towards future offerings; and
  » competition from elsewhere will have to compete on a full range of criteria in order to make inroads.

To date, Japanese manufacturing companies have concentrated on the axis economies of the EU, USA and their own domestic markets. Their presence in the EU has led to the capability to open up the states of the former USSR; and they are now also beginning to establish a presence elsewhere in Asia and also South America.

CONCLUSIONS

As stated in Chapter 1, there are few truly global organizations. It is clear that the numbers of organizations able to operate on a global basis is increasing as new markets open up, and because existing large companies with a history and experience of international operations are best placed to take immediate advantage.

There is a clear shift away from the political emphasis and influence. Once globalization was driven almost exclusively by political and military ambitions, supported by national economies. Now that many organizations have economic strength equivalent or greater than that of many nations, political drive and support is no longer necessary. Corporate empires on which "the sun never sets" now exist. These are set to increase in both size and influence as transport is further developed; as technological advance is driven by commercial rather than military and political priorities; and as, and when, e-commerce is developed as a genuinely profitable medium.

KEY LEARNING POINTS

The shift from political and military influences and ambition to commercial drives and priorities has brought:

» implications for levels of investment necessary for sustained commercial activity;
» changes to the nature of competition;
» behavioral lessons – especially those of the Romans, requiring positive attitudes to specific localities as a condition of long-term viability; and
» the development of technology, product, and service capacity and volume, so that it can be located anywhere with full effect.

The E-Dimension of Global Organizations

The Internet has great business and management potential for global organizations. This chapter explores the key issues, including security, and management capability, and organization structure and development.

INTRODUCTION

The worldwide Web and Internet have opened up global access to products, services, and information. This is perceived to greatly enhance business potential. It provides great potential for the management of organizations. Staff, customers and clients are accessible instantly, regardless of location or hour of the day. This is supported by the more or less universal availability of portable and laptop computers and mobile phone technology, itself improving in capacity and usability all the time, as well as reducing in price.

BUSINESS POTENTIAL

The rapid expansion of the worldwide Web and Internet over the last decade of the twentieth century led many to assume that this would now become the primary medium in which business was conducted. Investors rushed to place their money in virtual business ventures (dot.com companies). Supply side and distribution costs would be greatly reduced; there would also be a reduction in the fixed costs and charges necessary to run physical locations and traditional premises.

Both corporate and individual investors were drawn in (see summary box 3.2, Chapter 3). However, it quickly became apparent that the medium, while of great intrinsic interest, as well as being extremely fashionable, had not yet been sufficiently developed to provide a truly viable marketplace in most cases. The immediate consequence was heavy losses in stock values, and this hit both corporate and individual investors, as well as confidence in the medium as a marketplace, at least in the ways that it is structured at present. It is clear that:

» the existence of a Website that is globally accessible does not *per se* make a global organization; and
» intrinsic interest in the Web or Websites does not readily translate into commercially viable business. Extensive surfing of the Web, from both a personal and corporate point of view, is little more than browsing or window shopping *until* attention and interest are turned into desire and action (see summary box 4.1).

SUMMARY BOX 4.1: DOT.COM COMPANIES

Many of the original waves of dot.com companies found that, despite a global Website presence, in practice they could only conduct effective business in their own locality.

For example, boo.com, the Swedish Internet footwear retailer, found that supplying outside Northern Europe was neither viable from a delivery point of view, nor were individual transactions profitable. The company was effectively a local player only, using the Internet rather than a traditional retail outlet.

The company ran into difficulties when consumer interest could not be converted into purchases on a commercially viable scale. These difficulties were compounded by:

» the scale of capital employed ($160 million) on which returns were required;
» the lack of physical support. There was no facility for customer liaison, handling customer complaints or returning and exchanging wrongly dispatched goods until shortly before the firm closed down; and
» while the Website gave the company a global presence, there was no history or tradition of people from elsewhere in the world buying their shoes from Sweden. If people wanted shoes, they went out and bought them rather than logging on; and for the first time, the view was advanced that trade had strong behavioral aspects, rather than a single basis in convenience.

At present therefore, no clear focus exists for the development of the Web as a fully viable location of activities. Above all, no-one has yet transformed their business into one that is truly global as the result of Web usage or presence.

SECURITY

Website security remains a concern. Part of this is perceptual – many customers are unwilling to put their banking and credit card details on Websites for fear that they will subsequently be made public or else hacked into without authorization. This has led many Website operators to provide telephone lines alongside the Web provision so that this problem is alleviated.

This also reinforces the key concern that ultimately products and services have to be made available in the ways desired by customers, consumers and clients. However secure specific Websites may actually be, if customers do not believe or perceive this, they will not do business. This problem is compounded when customers know that they are giving details to Web companies located far away from their own place of residence. It underlines the subjectivity of buyer behavior elsewhere in the world.

These perceptions have been reinforced by two further elements: high profile hacking into government, corporate and public service Websites (e.g. two teenagers hacked into the Pentagon intranet in 1997). Also many organizations and police scrutinize their own internal Website and e-mail usage and content; and if the technology exists to do this on an official and open basis, it must be available to those with other purposes.

MANAGEMENT CAPABILITY

The Web has great value in enhancing all aspects of management practice provided that:

» it is used in support of the overarching prevailing organization and management principles and practices; and
» it is used as a medium to support and reinforce corporate communications rather than as a substitute.

Certainly, it makes possible corporate information flows to all staff regardless of location. Whatever business is being conducted anywhere in the world can be notified, reinforced and supported. Virtual communications can be designed to enhance and improve corporate cohesion, reporting relations and spans of control, whatever the location of individual activities.

It has specific usage in most areas of industrial and commercial activity. For example:

» *Professional and consulting services* – detailed proposals can be drawn up and, where necessary, referred back to headquarters for immediate approval or amendment.

» *Contract tendering* – for civil and other engineering and information technology projects, specifications can be produced and agreed anywhere in the world for any customer or client; and again, headquarters approval can be sought instantly when required.

» *Procedures* – management style, practice and decision-making can be reinforced anywhere in the world; and again, specific problems referred for decision in short order.

» *Product and service ranges* – these can be enhanced or developed much more quickly.

» *Customer and client management* – the Web and electronic information systems can be used as the basis for resolving disputes, agreeing to proposals and projects, and reinforcing general customer and client liaison; though these should always be reinforced and delivered face-to-face.

» *Supply side* – agreement on supply side arrangements can be reached at the point at which the purchaser visits the supplier's factory, quarry, premises, Website or database; and again, any disputes or areas of disagreement can be resolved on the spot.

More generally, Website, Internet and intranet usage reinforce management approaches, style and priorities. The content and priorities in management information systems establish and reinforce corporate culture, attitudes and values, and the actual priorities of the organization.

Website presence is one form of both internal and external marketing. The presentation, content, quality and usability of sites all reinforce general images, attitudes to staff, customers, clients, and suppliers, as well as holding information that can be downloaded.

SUPERVISION

Use of e-mail and the Web enables a form of supervision of operations in remote locations. To be fully effective, this must be supported, as far as possible, by physical presence. It is of particular value to regional and local offices that, in global organizations, have the primary function of acting as a conduit of information between headquarters and frontline activities. Used as a support function, it is an extremely effective element of organization structures based on regional headquarters and localized activities. Where necessary, it can be used as the vehicle by which effective reporting relations are developed; and in some cases, this is the main part of the process. Again, this requires supporting through visibility and observed and actual practice. Even when physical meetings are intermittent or irregular, these set the tone for the actual relationship and management and supervisory style; the e-contact develops and reinforces this rather than countering or diluting it (see summary box 4.2).

SUMMARY BOX 4.2: CIVIL ENGINEERING IN KAZAKHSTAN

A team of UK civil engineering consultants working in Kazakhstan was sent to negotiate with the government of that country on the possibility and feasibility of developing the water distribution infrastructure. The company had already carried out some small but specialized work; local officials held them in high respect; and the next round of work needed doing. The team produced an outline feasibility document. They checked it with their London headquarters, which told them to go ahead and plan in more detail.

Everyone was happy. The negotiations went on for a further three months. At the end of the period, a detailed proposal was agreed, including costings, timescales and local labor and materials content. The company would be paid in dollars and the work was underwritten by an EU support program.

The team took time and trouble to get to know and understand the local culture and how the officials with influence thought and behaved. The result was mutual confidence and high expectations. The team reported to headquarters that the proposal was now ready for signing.

The company flew its projects director to the location. Having approved the proposal by e-dimension, he now demanded to see all the papers. He then went through these with a red pen making substantial alterations. He demanded to see the local officials, whom he tried to browbeat into accepting his changes.

The local officials refused and the deal was cancelled. The projects director flew back to London where he instituted disciplinary proceedings against the consulting team leader. He was however, forced to backtrack. He was later transferred to other duties when it became apparent that he had neither read nor understood the proposal when it was first sent to him through the e-dimension; and that he had only kept the team in Kazakhstan at all for the perceived prestige that accrued at headquarters.

The initial contract value was $47 million with the clear prospect of more to follow.

Where staff are located in remote parts, it may be necessary to alter the priorities of headquarters' managers to ensure that the visible aspects are developed. This means requiring senior and regional managers to undertake regular visits to such places, as well as ensuring that remote staff come into headquarters or regional offices at some point during periods of leave. However well developed the e-supervision, ultimately it depends on the physical style adopted.

MANAGEMENT AND STAFF DEVELOPMENT

The e-dimension has great potential as management and staff training support. This again requires integration with the core physical effort. It has little value conducted in isolation.

Most organizations have the following.

» *Induction and core training programs* – setting overall standards of attitude, behavior and performance, and providing initial bodies of information about the particular organization; and setting clear standards in health and safety, emergency procedures and initial job training and orientation.
» *Staff development programs* – based on a combination of personal, occupational, organizational and professional drives and requirements; and collective and individual responsibilities for enhancing expertise and developing potential.
» *Project work and secondments* – in which groups and individuals are assigned to specific problems, issues or locations for reasons stated at the outset.

» *Specific activities* – agreed at performance review and appraisal, and which have to be carried out somehow.

Each has great potential for effectiveness and development through Website material. Organization information can be universally provided everywhere in the world; and specific, often sensitive, areas of the Website accessed through the use of security codes and passwords. Again however, the true value is only realized if it is fully integrated with physical, organizational and managerial support. Whatever the quality of Website offering, the following should be addressed.

» Induction, orientation and core training programs require a leader who is present. This person must speak with the full authority of the organization and be able to answer specific questions, as well as providing a physical reflection of behavior, attitudes and values.
» Supporting information for staff development programs can be placed on Websites; and for those in remote locations, this may become a driving force. It is essential that, from time to time, those on these programs are brought together with a tutor, leader or facilitator. It is equally essential that e-contacts are available in between physical meetings. Failure to do this dilutes the learning and development effort. Otherwise, whether or not the case, it becomes known, believed and perceived that the virtual approach is a substitute for real and substantial activity. There then becomes no positive reason to log on to the particular program and participants begin to drift away (see summary box 4.3).

SUMMARY BOX 4.3: THE PERCEPTION OF E-LEARNING

From the point of view of organizations and learning and training providers, the e-dimension is initially very attractive. Universally accessible, and without the need for extensive classroom facility and tutor provision, to the unwary this may seem fully cost effective.

This is invariably perceived as cheap at the receiving end. Nobody likes to be associated with cheapness because it is demeaning and dilutes self-worth. Such programs are normally commissioned by those who have learned either through practical experience or physical attendance at business school. There is therefore no empathy for the process, even if there is some understanding of the potential.

ORGANIZATION STRUCTURE DEVELOPMENT

Global organizations require extensive networks of suppliers, distributors, specialists, consultants, subcontractors and local partners. Properly used, the e-dimension provides for quick and effective communications, consultation and decision-making, and the potential for universal availability of information across the entire organization and its networks. Those on the supply side can be asked to consider their provision from a position of full understanding of the finished product or service. This applies to those at each stage along the way. Local partners can identify cultural or operational differences that may have been taken for granted or missed altogether by the global organizations.

Language

Language barriers require managing and this is a matter of corporate policy (see summary box 4.4).

SUMMARY BOX 4.4: LANGUAGE BARRIER EXAMPLES

» *Eurotunnel*, the company that commissioned the building of the channel tunnel between the south-east of the UK and the north-east of France, required all its staff to be prepared, willing, and able to conduct strategy, policy, and operational meetings in either English or French.
» *Balfour-Beatty*, the UK civil engineering company, engaged a specialist tunneling contractor from Austria to advise on

and lead specialist operations during the construction of the Heathrow Airport underground link. When part of the tunnel collapsed Balfour-Beatty were prosecuted and fined $2 million. The company blamed part of the problem on the language and cultural barriers that existed between themselves and their subcontractor.

Both face-to-face and in the management of the e-dimension, direction is required on:

» whether the organization has a single language in which all those who work for it are required to be proficient; and
» whether the organization is prepared, willing, and able to accommodate language diversity without consequences to operations and activities.

The right answer is that decided upon for the particular organization or situation. It requires active consideration and a strategic decision. This is required to ensure uniformity and conformity, and also as the basis for buying the required technology and software.

Website and e-commerce software has to be led, designed and developed as a direct consequence, so that everything is both fully integrated and capable of universal access and understanding. Where local partners and other specialists are engaged who do not have the facility, this becomes an organization development and operational requirement. It is of critical importance where a long-term relationship is envisaged. At the outset, translation facilities are required. It may be necessary, again, to retain these on a longer-term basis where highly specialist and technical language is involved.

CONCLUSIONS

Those responsible for directing and managing global organizations have to realize and understand that the e-dimension is a major opportunity for the development of strategy, policy and operations, and enhancing the availability and quality of corporate, regional, and local management information and decision-making processes.

The e-dimension is not a substitute for any of these. It is an additional corporate responsibility, not a replacement for others. It is to reinforce management style and priorities rather than replace them. It requires full training, development and awareness, and this must include attention to limitations and what the technology cannot do, as well as the considerable opportunities afforded.

KEY LEARNING POINTS

The universal availability, access and ability to locate technology anywhere in the world has brought:

» universal availability and access to information; and
» the ability to locate production and service functions to optimum advantage at the organization's discretion.

This universal availability has, however, so far failed to overcome:

» language barriers;
» cultural barriers; and
» the need to match hardware, software and human capability.

It is also necessary to understand that a global website presence does not mean that the organization itself is global.

BEST PRACTICE CASE: ALODIS
Total support anywhere in the world

Alodis is a physical and virtual support network and federation of services provided to freelance and self-employed professionals wherever in the world they are working. It is owned by Mongrel World Ltd. based in London, UK, which provides a comprehensive range of support services, networks, contacts, hardware and software. Alodis' target population is:

» those who work as consultants, experts and specialists on a freelance basis for global organizations anywhere in the world;
» those in the UK (at present) who have to balance life and work demands including childcare and domestic priorities;

» those on fully flexible work patterns, portable careers, and portfolio activities; and

» recent graduates who are trying to make progress on a freelance or self-employed basis.

The parent company, Mongrel World, also acts as: "A voice for the under-represented providing them with services tailored to their needs and giving them a political voice."

Alodis' core services

These are:

» *Alodis Magazine* – which is published monthly, providing a wide range of features including profiles of successful entrepreneurs and professionals; the conduct of business in different parts of the world; reviews of software packages; self-conduct and self-presentation in different industries and commercial and public sectors across the world; lobbying governments and trade federations; providing a meeting point between multinational and global organizations and individual specialists.

» *Alodis assistants* – offering personal assistants who undertake diary management, message forwarding, travel arrangements, meeting schedules and business support anywhere in the world. This service is hired on a basis tailored to individual needs and wants. It is guaranteed to be available at whatever time that suits the individual.

» *Alodis.com* – the linchpin of the operation. Alodis.com enables everything required by those traveling for business anywhere in the world including the assistant service as indicated above; templates and schedules for business plans in particular locations; and especially the production of summaries, costings, logistics, time and distance issues in relation to the particular location. It provides comprehensive information on local networks, suppliers and the presence of specific expertise. The Website may be contacted at any time, on any issue at all. It has a referral system if either the query cannot be answered directly, or if the answer does not meet the particular individual's needs. It also provides emergency travel arrangements and timetable scheduling so that if the individual is held up, Alodis will change diaries, times and dates of meetings. Also provided are meeting arrangements at air and seaports, room and other facility bookings, and equipment and technology hire.

» *General management support services* – these remove the need for people to return to their home base except when it suits them. The next round of presentations, projects and activities can be scheduled using the present (rather than the home) location as the starting point, reducing traveling time and expense, and releasing these resources to increase the quality and value of future performance.

Conclusions

Alodis is based in London, UK, and take-up of its services is overwhelmingly British. The services are available always and everywhere to those who do use them.

It is a demonstration of the potential for the global development of fully flexible professional, technical, expert, and specialist operations. It also demonstrates how fully integrated networks and federations can be developed. As such, it has lessons and implications for larger organizations as they seek new markets and ways of working; and as they have an ever-increasing demand for the availability of individual and collective specialization and expertise at short notice, and for specific periods of time.

The Global Dimension

It is essential for global organizations to identify specific strategic and operational issues This chapter discusses investment, market, and locations and looks at a best practice case in Walmart Inc.

INTRODUCTION

It is essential to identify key specific strategic and operational issues. The nature and mix varies between organizations and within specific activities. Each has to be addressed from the point of view of gaining and maintaining a profitable and effective presence, and understanding, accepting, and managing the consequent responsibilities.

INVESTMENT

The following views presently prevail.

Long-term and enduring

This is the approach adopted by Japanese manufacturing companies when establishing elsewhere in the world. It requires attending to, and underwriting, every aspect of new business development.

The companies required "green-field" sites in areas of high unemployment because they wanted to be able to design their own infrastructure, access, and egress, as well as having access to large potential pools of labor. Investment therefore had to cover:

» full costings, evaluation, and feasibility of many sites from which one would be chosen;
» cultural, social, and economic analyses of each site in order to understand the corporate responsibilities for fitting into the local communities;
» plant and technology assessment, related to size, scope, and scale; and therefore, in turn, to the size and nature of the local population and workforce required. Almost universally, the companies accepted full responsibility for training and development of the workforce from scratch. This presently extends to product, service, and technological updates to ensure fully flexible operations, long-term production optimization, and the ability to upgrade and transform both expertise and equipment when required;
» new product and service development as opportunities became apparent, and as local knowledge and understanding led to a deeper comprehension of where sustainable competitive advantage truly lay; and

» enhanced cultural understanding leading to further capability in assessing the barriers that exist in particular markets, sectors and locations (see summary box 5.1).

SUMMARY BOX 5.1: CULTURAL BARRIERS

Japanese companies operating in the EU have had less success in market penetration in France and Italy than elsewhere. This is because the population of those countries continues to exhibit high levels of "nationalist affinity" with local products and producers: Fiat, Citroen, Peugeot, Renault (cars); Thomson, Zanussi (electrical and white goods). As a consequence of this, Toyota has engaged in partnership with Renault in order to gain a foothold rather than trying to develop its own independent market.

Similarly, when McDonald's first entered France, they found themselves having to develop their own new markets rather than competing for existing customers with the local provision. To date, approximately 50 per cent of McDonald's turnover in France is generated by tourists, rather than the indigenous population. This may be compared with the UK, where only 10 per cent of turnover is generated by tourists. Most of this is in London. In the whole of the UK, McDonald's has established a much firmer indigenous market than in France.

Short-term

The levels of finance commanded by many global organizations have enabled them to take strategic investment decisions based on the ability to relocate quickly if operational circumstances or other prevailing conditions change. Japanese companies have brought down their investment appraisal processes from between two and three years to between three and six months; and in more volatile industries (e.g. garment manufacture, sports goods, food processing) the process of decision-making in terms of location may only take a few days. This has enabled organizations to make strategic changes, especially on the supply side, in very short order (see summary box 5.2).

SUMMARY BOX 5.2: GARMENT MANUFACTURE

Only 15 per cent of garments sold in Western markets are manufactured in the USA, EU or Japan. This is because there is an enormous pool of cheap labor in the third world and the required technology is more or less universally available.

High brand manufacturers (e.g. Nike, Reebok, The Gap) have, from time to time, attracted attention from those concerned about the conditions in which those who work in the factories are kept, and the extreme low levels of pay and harsh terms and conditions of employment.

This is not confined to these companies however. Marks & Spencer, the UK department store chain, founded, developed, and managed on very high standards of ethical conduct, unilaterally cancelled supply contracts with Scottish garment manufacturers at 24 hours notice, announcing that it too would now be sourcing this part of its activities in rural south-east Asia. At the time, the company was going through severe commercial difficulties. The adverse publicity about the decision to relocate the supply side compounded, rather than alleviated, the problems. The company also had no history of trading with the Far East. It was not (and is not) a global organization. The inescapable conclusion therefore was that this decision had been taken as a matter of expediency, rather than based on full understanding of this form of trading.

Short-term capability makes it easy to switch locations for any reason. These include quality of product and the nature of the business relationship. It also means that changes can be made for reasons of expediency as the result of adverse publicity in one location or to avoid the prying eyes of investigative journalists.

Global organizations and MNCs have also found themselves able to enhance returns on investments by ordering suppliers either to cut costs or enhance production volumes in the contract price. Morally repugnant, it nevertheless enhances short-term returns and is a key feature of cost management in many large and dominant organizations.

Profits

Whatever the attitude to investment policy, returns on investment and profits have to be managed. This is driven by understanding the following.

» Returns on investment and profit margins vary both between, and within, sectors. For example, positive returns on grocery sales in the USA are approximately one to three per cent per annum; in the UK 10 per cent per annum is expected. Organizations that wish to develop their core business in other parts of the world either have to accept that the returns may, and do, vary, or else invest further in market development in order to gain the margins desired.

» Dumping and flooding. In pursuit of this, some organizations have resorted to product service and market dumping and flooding. Initially large volumes of product or service are made available at prices advantageous to the local market, and indigenous providers are driven out. Prices are then subsequently raised, both for repeat sales and new business development. The local market has then the choice either to pay the new prices, or else forego the products, services and benefits on offer.

Such policies are only sustainable until new players enter with their own cost and price advantages. However, this often takes several years; and in many cases, the cycle tends to repeat itself.

Price levels

Other approaches include the formation of cartels (price fixing arrangements) and market allocations (whereby major players agree not to encroach on each other's territories). Cartels and allocations are illegal in the EU, Australia, New Zealand and some states of the USA. In practice, the prices charged for differentiated homogenous products and services are often very similar in these locations as elsewhere. This helps in initial and continuous assessment of market, product and service values and duration; it is a short step from this to market domination and unacceptable levels of profiteering.

Establishing independent pricing policies is driven by the need to generate the desired returns on investment. The extent to which particular returns are possible should ideally be conducted on the basis of what the market can bear in absolute terms, as well as current levels. This is because if circumstances change, then both market structure and returns have to be reassessed. In this context, the following specific issues can then be addressed.

» The need to recover variable costs (the costs of production, sales, output and distribution). Global organizations and MNCs approach this through a combination of:

  » cross-subsidy, whereby losses or reduced margins in one location are subsidized by high surpluses in others. It is normally necessary to address this from a strategic point of view. For example, closing down individual loss making operations may induce perceptions that the company is no longer global, and this may have repercussions for stock values, as well as customer perceptions; and

  » transfer pricing, in which income is assessed in the currency of the company's choice. This is usually either the local currency, or dollars or euros.

» The need to maintain a global presence to ensure that perceptions are fully reinforced; and so that local operations can be structured in order that effective specific locations can be sustained.

» The need to open new markets and to develop expertise in pricing as these opportunities unfold.

» Moral aspects which are a matter of corporate responsibility in which a balance is struck between the ability to make particular charges, and what is right and wrong in the circumstances. High levels of charges are possible for essential supplies in deregulated markets, e.g. property (UK); energy (western world and Japan); while low levels can be imposed on those who need the trade to survive, e.g. oil (Africa); hardwoods (Malaysia); minerals (former USSR, Central and southern Africa).

» Governments and other sources of public finance and the value that this truly carries. Global organizations may become involved in locations and markets as the result of inducements, tax breaks or guaranteed further contracts. To be fully effective in the long-term, a genuine commercial advantage must either exist, or be provided (see summary box 5.3).

SUMMARY BOX 5.3: GOVERNMENTS AND PUBLIC FINANCE INDUCEMENTS

Following the collapse of the former USSR, the World Bank, the World Trade Organization, the EU, and the USA sought contracts for the restructuring of the newly independent member states. Civil engineering and other infrastructure development projects were commissioned and it was widely anticipated that commercial services would follow. Everything was initially underwritten by EU, USA and World Bank guarantees. Success was therefore perceived to be assured.

Strategic and operational problems started almost immediately. Nobody involved considered the effects of the consequent social and political upheaval. The Red Army (then the largest organization in the world) had not been paid for months. There was a thriving black market and a burgeoning and well-organized mafia. Western experts, officials and contractors became targets for kidnapping and extortion. No project could be undertaken without the payment of protection money to local gangsters and warlords; and this had to be paid in dollars (the rouble collapsed from dollar parity to 1:1200 in four years).

Matters came to a head when an $11 billion dollar World Bank loan to the Russian government vanished without trace during 1996–98. Shortly afterwards, an oil engineering crew working in Chechnya was kidnapped by local rebels. This group demanded their ransom. This was not forthcoming, and when the Red Army went in to crush the rebellion, the members of the oil engineering crew were beheaded.

MARKETS AND LOCATIONS

The key to enduring, successful, effective, and profitable global performance lies in understanding every market in which activities are either being considered or presently undertaken (see summary box 5.4).

SUMMARY BOX 5.4: MARKET KNOWLEDGE AND UNDERSTANDING

Part of the initial resentment against Japanese manufacturing incursions into hitherto protected Western markets in the 1970s and 1980s lay in the fact that they had taken so much time and effort in understanding the precise nature and demands of the new markets. In many cases, they built up more detailed profiles of customer and client bases than anything thus far achieved by the indigenous providers who tended to take on trust the perception that their local history, presence and provision would secure them against all competition.

In many cases also, those that worked on these assumptions assumed that they would automatically receive a favorable welcome when they tried to trade elsewhere in the world without any market research, testing or understanding. Early consignments of UK cars shipped to Japan could not be run on the local fuel provision, nor did they meet exhaust emission regulations. When early attempts were made to establish markets for electrical goods from the UK, EU and USA they were found not to work from the Japanese national grid.

This is from the point of view of the following.

» Size and volume; propensity to spend; the position of the particular products and services *in the priority order of the particular market itself*.
» The strength of existing provision, whether local, international or provided by a global organization.
» The benefits brought by the proposed new player.
» The conditions necessary to establish reputation, substantial products and services, and returns required.
» Background work, market appraisal and research required.
» Access and egress of products and services if they are not to be produced on the spot; access and egress of components, raw materials and databases if they are.

» Testing assumptions and organizational received wisdom rather than taking potential markets and opportunities for granted (see summary box 5.5).

SUMMARY BOX 5.5: THE CONSEQUENCE OF TAKING THINGS FOR GRANTED

A firm of global management consultants was engaged by a large UK civil engineering contractor. This company regularly described itself as "global" in its own documentation. Over the past 50 years, the company had worked in a total of 33 countries. Overall, 90 per cent of revenues were accrued from UK-based operations and activities. Of the company's 15 regional offices, 13 were in the UK in different locations, one was in the eastern USA, and the other in Kuala Lumpur, Malaysia.

The company asked the consultants for a briefing on how to maximize civil engineering opportunities that were to accrue to it from the opening up of the Vietnamese coastline to oil prospecting and exploration.

The consultants asked the senior projects manager whether the company had conducted their own feasibility studies, assessed local labor markets, operating conditions, access to materials, or returns available. No, came the answer, but since the company was a global player, none of this mattered.

One of the consultants then asked the senior projects manager to name 10 UK civil engineering companies. This, he did. He was then asked to name 10 Asian civil engineering companies. This, he failed to do. The consultant then said: "That is fair enough. You have not heard of them; and they will not have heard of you."

To date, the company has made no incursion into the Vietnamese or any other Far Eastern market; nor is it willing to undertake the investment or research necessary to do so.

Ensuring effective and profitable global performance can then be further considered as follows.

» Whether to provide universal products and services for which global market demand can be generated.

» Whether to provide distinctive local variations of core products and services; and whether to develop distinctive local markets in peripheral or derived products and services.

» Whether to be driven purely by the market, using economies of scale and sheer financial size to become involved in anything that the particular location wants or needs.

Whichever standpoint is adopted, the decision to proceed is then fully informed and the desired state of the activity can be developed and implemented.

CONCLUSIONS

Whatever the markets, products, and services of projects contemplated, global organizations have to attend to universal aspects of investment appraisal and assessment, the viability of operations, and the demands of specific locations.

It should also be clear that specialist expertise may have to be engaged as a part of the investment process – however familiar the particular location may seem to be. Global organizations can lose a substantial part of their reputation through lack of attention to well known and supposedly understood areas because they cease to consider their own locality in the same rigorous ways in which they assess prospects located in remote parts of the world.

KEY LEARNING POINTS

The key to effective globalization is the identification of a determined and pre-designed strategic position. Specific attention is then required to:

» investment strategy;
» costs and returns, including pricing policies and internal approaches to charging;
» the relationship between global organizations and governments, and other public institutions and providers of finance;
» market and location assessment; and
» the nature of returns available in specific sectors and locations.

BEST PRACTICE CASE: WALMART INC.

Introduction

Walmart Inc. is the largest retailer in the world. It is founded on the basis of being the largest US mass and discount retailer with 2500 stores and year 2000 revenues of $165 billion.

Founded in Bentonville, Arkansas, in 1946, the company has grown to its present state through strategies of planned expansion, first in the US, and subsequently overseas. Walmart finally achieved a presence in all 50 states when it opened its first operation in Vermont in 1995. It has subsequently developed extensive operations in Canada and Korea, as well as having strategies for expansion in the EU and elsewhere.

The takeover of Asda in the UK

In 1998, Walmart bought Asda, the third largest UK retailer, as part of its program of planned expansion. The move was welcomed by a wide range of interests in the UK.

» *Customers and consumer groups* – had been lobbying government and trade federations for many years to bring food and consumer goods prices down. Comparisons produced by the National Consumers Council, and other interest groups, universally concluded that prices for products and services available at supermarkets were higher than in the rest of the EU, and much higher than North America. Walmart's takeover of Asda was accompanied by extensive media coverage. This drew favorable attention to Walmart's perceived practice of "pile it high, sell it cheap." Individual consumers were flown to random locations in the United States to produce "basket of goods" comparisons that demonstrated that prices charged in the USA were up to 60 per cent cheaper than the UK.

» *Political interests* – the move received overt support from the government and the acquisition was allowed to proceed unopposed by the UK Mergers and Competition Commission. The collective view was that global barriers were being broken down in many sectors already and there was no reason why this should not extend to groceries and consumer goods in the interest of extending choice. Over 90 per cent of UK grocery and consumer goods retailing would still be directed and operated from the UK because Asda only had seven per cent of the market. Also politically it was "a good thing" to be seen to be encouraging lower prices and a wide range of choice.

» *Suppliers* – welcomed the move because of squeezes placed on them by the existing players. Walmart was known to have its own sources and to be extremely stringent in terms of price, quality, value, volume, and delivery. However, their program of planned expansion and existing site development would provide major opportunities for those willing to do things the Walmart way.

Conclusions

The move by Walmart into the UK was consequently welcomed all round. The only exceptions were small independent retailers who perceived that their margins would be squeezed further, and that many would be forced out of business. Academic interests also questioned whether the Walmart strategy would deliver American prices to European markets; or whether (as for example, in the case of Euro-Disney) the company would seek to take advantage of the higher prices that European consumers were willing to pay.

Since the takeover, there have been short bouts of "price warring" in the sector, especially between Walmart/Asda and Tesco, the largest indigenous operator. However, the retail prices index for grocery and supermarket products in the UK continues to rise at a steady two to three per cent per annum, and gross profit margins continue at 10 per cent per annum as distinct from the three per cent per annum generated by Walmart through its US operations.

The State of the Art of Global Organizations

Global organizations are constantly evolving and their successful and profitable management depends on continued attention to several key elements. This chapter examines:

» strategy;
» marketing;
» financial management;
» organization structures and cultures; and
» environment management.

INTRODUCTION

The effective, successful and profitable management of global organizations depends on continued attention to, and development of, a number of key elements along the lines demanded by the size, scope, scale and location of activities, and the pressures of particular markets. Specific attention is required in all cases to the following.

» The physical and psychological management of distance. The former includes the relationship between the location of activities, headquarters and regional offices, and management structures; the latter requires attention to the perceptual and behavioral barriers that exist between different locations, global organizations and their markets, and known, believed and perceived status and priority differentials in different work groups and locations.

» Maintaining and developing cost, resource, and competitive advantages in all locations; and monitoring and developing the economies of scope and scale necessary to secure a truly global position (see summary box 6.1).

SUMMARY BOX 6.1: MERGERS AND TAKEOVERS

Major driving forces behind mergers and acquisition strategies are the ability to develop a global presence relatively quickly; and the perceived ability through acquisition to consolidate resource bases.

About 90 per cent of mergers and takeovers fail or fall short of full success. This is because the entire venture is driven by resource and location requirements, and short-term stock advantages. Insufficient attention is paid to cultural barriers, management style suitability, technological and infrastructure compatibility, and the management of subsequent merged or acquired operations and activities.

Sources: Institute of Management (UK) (2000) "Mergers and Acquisitions"; American Management Association (2000) "The Advantages and Consequences of Acquisition Strategies."

STRATEGY

Harvard Business School's *Michael Porter* (1980) states that to be successful in commercial activities, a generic strategic position is required. One of the following is essential.

» *Cost leadership* – the drive to be the lowest cost operator in the field. This enables the absolute ability to compete on price where necessary; where this is not necessary, high levels of sustainable profit are achieved in both absolute terms and also in relation to competitors. For cost leadership, investment is required in current production technology and high quality staff.
» *Focus* – concentrating on niches and taking steps to be indispensable. The purpose is to establish a long-term and concentrated relationship with distinctive customers based on product and service confidence, high levels of quality, complete reliability and the ability to produce and deliver product and service volumes when required.
» *Differentiation* – offering homogenous products on the basis of creating a strong image or identity based on marketing, advertising, brand development, strength and loyalty, and outlets and distribution.

Porter (2001) develops this further, stating that whatever the location of activities, size or operations of organizations, the principle of the established generic strategy must be upheld. Referring specifically to the use of the Internet as a foum for the conduct of business, as well as to globalization, he states: "There are no new business models. Whatever is contemplated must be capable of persuading customers to use your product or service in preference to all alternatives."

Global organizations and large MNCs have to additionally consider their generic position as follows.

» Whether to drive for cost advantages in all markets and locations, or to adopt different generic positions for each (cost leaders).
» Whether to concentrate on developing products and services to satisfy the existing customer and client base; or whether to seek new niches for the existing range of offerings (focus).

» How to differentiate effectively in all locations and markets served, images, packaging and branding desired and required (differentiation).

» Whether to offer "country of origin" products and services everywhere on the basis that any local market can be developed anywhere in the world; or whether to produce fully localized products and services according to known, understood and perceived locality demands, needs, and wants.

» How to make the generic position work to best advantage in order to sustain a competitive position in specific locations. At present, the overwhelming majority of global organizations and large MNCs are from "axis economies" (see Table. 6.1).

Table 6.1 The World's 500 Largest Corporations. (Source: "The Fortune Global 500", 2001.).

Country/block	No. of multinational corporations
United States	162
European Union	155
Japan	126
Switzerland	14
South Korea	13
Canada	6
Brazil	5
Australia	5
China	3
Other	11

Wherever the location of activities, ventures are more or less certain to be financed by US, EU or Japanese backers and these will have their demands and expectations from particular markets, as well as from the organization overall. The primary concern therefore becomes the returns on particular ventures, and whatever generic position is adopted has to satisfy this interest. The fact that the financial interest can be satisfied in one location does not mean that the same will occur in others (see summary box 6.2).

SUMMARY BOX 6.2: STRATEGIES AND FAILURE

Failure is more or less certain to occur if the following conditions are present.

» Increased price/standard value of product or service.
» Increased price/low value of product or service (only sustainable by monopolies or oligopolies).
» Standard price/low value (immediate threat from potential entrants).
» Standard price/variable value in closely located markets.
» Lack of identity, perception or understanding of product and service benefits.
» Lack of understanding, acceptance, and perceived value of products and services.
» Getting the price, quality, value balance wrong in specific markets and locations.
» Differential pricing in markets accessible by single consumer groups.
» Differential pricing in public services.
» Differential pricing in industrial and commercial services (e.g. management and other specialist consultancy and expertise; technology, equipment, and software supplies).

MARKETING

Marketing has to be engaged on a truly competitive basis whatever the location or nature of products or services. For global organizations, marketing is likely to reflect competition with local providers and with other MNCs. Attention is therefore required to:

» *Substance* – the price, quality, value, and benefits mix of what is on offer and afforded to the particular sector or location; and whether the particular sector or location values these.
» *Presentation* – the images, packaging, design, and appearance of the product or service; brochure and other presentations of services; and the extent to which each element reflects the aspirations and desires for association of the particular sector or location.

The requirement is to be able to generate an actively loyal customer base regardless of location and this requires extensive customer research and understanding.

Customers

Customers may be defined as the follows.

» Apostles – demonstrating super-loyalty to the organization, products, and services.
» Loyalists – those who keep returning to the organization for products and services.
» Mercenaries – who choose products and services on price and convenience.
» Hostages and captives – who use the organization's products and services because there is no choice; unwary organizations often come to view hostages as loyalists, and are consequently deeply disappointed when they lose large volumes to competitors entering the market.
» Defectors – those who used to be customers of the organization.
» Terrorists – those who have received bad service or products from the organization and who take active steps to communicate this to the rest of the world.

Product and service flooding and dumping may drive other producers out of particular sectors leaving customers with little choice but to use what is now available. The best that this produces is an "active captive" customer and client base. Customers only continue to do business because they need or want the benefits of what is on offer. They will change their habits as soon as there is a genuine alternative.

Images

In the axis economies, the strongest images remain:

» sex, especially sexual presentations of the female form;
» youth;
» glamour;
» vitality;
» security and comfort (e.g. safety features in cars; psychological security reflected in images of stable family life in consumer goods advertising);

» strong colors, especially the use of red, black, purple, maroon, deep blue; and

» sunshine and warmth.

Market research in particular locations must produce a full understanding of:

» images, packaging, presentation, and advertising that are acceptable in particular locations, whether or not these reflect the values of the axis economies;

» images that are unacceptable; and

» strong and weak themes.

From this comes the basis of attraction and interest; and the potential for product and service desire, purchase, usage – and repeat purchase and usage.

To be fully effective, this requires substantial local input. Attempts to impose axis products, services, and images may succeed in the short to medium-term, especially if reinforced with flooding and dumping. To secure the long-term, customers and clients have to be comfortable in their own terms with what they are buying, using, and consuming and also with the consequent associations and identity (see summary box 6.3).

SUMMARY BOX 6.3: NEWLY INDEPENDENT STATES

Following the collapse of communism in 1988-91, the western states of the former USSR looked forward to liberal democracies, consumer booms, and the opportunity to enjoy the lifestyles hitherto only available in the USA and EU. The Czech Republic, Poland, Hungary, Slovakia and others all rushed in their applications to join the EU. US and EU MNCs were quick to establish in these countries, bringing Western products and services.

Some disillusion has subsequently set in. Initial enthusiasm has been tempered by the reality that:

» politically, the EU requires structural, industrial, commercial and public service reforms led by Western interests and which have driven unemployment up to fifteen or twenty per cent;

» commercial footholds established by Western MNCs have been for the benefit of their own headquarters rather than the new locations; and

» Western style and standard consumer goods are priced too high for much of the population; and Western organizations have targeted their products and services at those who can afford them without consideration of those who cannot.

Both at the macro and micro levels therefore, presentation, expectations, and reality are seriously at variance from each other. Western companies are plainly doing things their way, and are perceived and understood by the majority of consumers in the ex-communist states to have nothing to offer to the majority of the population unless they are willing to pay substantial percentages of their low levels of income in order to acquire them.

Products and services

Decisions can then be taken on which customers to serve, when, where, and for how long; and how to go about attracting them. This also must be underwritten by extensive research. The most successful global organizations present a combination of inherent product or service strength and advantage, with local and targeted packaging, presentation, images, price ranges, and other aspects of the marketing mix demanded by particular sectors (see summary box 6.4).

SUMMARY BOX 6.4: SECTOR AND LOCATION MARKETING

Local and regional offices are ideally established in order to make major contributions to marketing, market development, and assessment of potential. In particular, this means the constant testing of assumptions usually made by headquarters in the land of origin.

Many UK and US MNCs fully understand the substantial regional differences between New York city and Buffalo (New York State, USA), or London and Manchester (UK), without developing the same line of reasoning to make equivalent assessments in different parts of the world. For example, there are substantial differences between Johannesburg and Cape Town (South Africa), Hanoi and Saigon (Vietnam), Rio de Janeiro and Sao Paolo (Brazil); and failure to address these is likely to lead to long-term failure in regional policies.

Entry barriers

Global organizations and large MNCs are not normally faced with entry barriers that cannot be surmounted. The only exception is a lack of full understanding of the market and nature of activities required. Where things do go wrong, organizational and managerial problems can often be overcome by sheer economic size and strength, especially if this has been sufficient to see them through difficulties in the past. Access to supplies, technology, and expertise is not normally an issue. Effective application in particular situations is a problem if high levels of broad understanding are not first achieved. Global organizations have the strength to take over local providers as a quick, and potentially effective, means of market entry; problems are caused when the local provider's strengths are swamped by the preconceptions of the new owners.

Exit barriers

Similarly, global organizations can normally withdraw at short notice from activities without lasting damage to themselves, at least in the short-term. However, issues are certain to arise if factories have to be closed because of changes in sourcing policies or if waste and effluent is left behind causing potential health hazards. This is bad long-term marketing and causes future incomers to be viewed with mistrust. It may also lead to resistance in new markets and other locations if adverse publicity accrues as the result.

Global organizational marketing therefore depends for enduring effectiveness on implementing and developing relationships that are capable of mutual understanding and profitability in terms positively acceptable to all concerned. Marketing policies based on expediency, flooding, dominance, and the ability to flout entry and exit barriers may create a short to medium-term advantage. Such policies are not fully sustainable in the long-term.

FINANCIAL MANAGEMENT

Global organization financial management is concerned with the following.

» Stock values and capital structure, large enough to fund and underwrite ventures anywhere in the world, and stable enough to bear problems of currency fluctuations.

» Revenue streams in a variety of currencies, which may, or may not, be useful for translating into hard currencies or that of the country of origin.

» Revenue management in which decisions are required whether to fund operations in particular areas in local or hard currency, or that of the country of origin.

» Revenue hedging in which currencies are bought and sold as commodities as a hedge against sudden sharp losses or increases in value.

» Revenue risk management requiring assessment of all activities on an individual and corporate basis from the following points of view:

   » sectoral trends: whether growing or declining either in size or prosperity;

   » social, political, and economic issues: including currency fluctuations and the prospect of local currency collapses;

   » factors inside and outside the control of the organization and its managers;

   » the structure of operations and the financial decisions attached to them; and

   » the ability to develop and generate forecasting expertise so that both economic and political volatility can be predicted with a fair degree of certainty.

Global organizations require the capability to spread risk so that if financial conditions in one area do deteriorate, these can be underwritten by strengths in others. This, in turn, requires systems of local, regional and corporate reporting relationships. Management information systems must be capable of up-to-the-minute situational and market assessment, and informing short-term strategic financial movements as and when required.

However global an organization may be, its sources of capital are overwhelmingly likely to be domestic. Opportunities that appear certain winners to backers in the axis or country of origin may not be so on the ground in remote parts of the world. A key part of global organization financial management is therefore the capability to brief and educate financiers, stockbrokers, shareholders, backers, and their representatives. It is necessary also to ensure that coverage in the financial and other media is actively informed (see summary box 6.5).

SUMMARY BOX 6.5: FINANCIAL MANAGEMENT AND MEDIA INFLUENCE

The importance of engaging in active and productive contact with the financial media cannot be overstated. For example:

"Economists may sometimes be seen about as useful as a chocolate teapot but as this year's Nobel Prize for economics shows, it is not always so. On October 14, the $1 million Nobel Prize for economics was awarded to two Americans, Robert Merton of Harvard University and Myron Scholes of Stamford University. Their prize-winning work involved precisely the sort of mind-boggling mathematical formulae that usually cause non-economists either to snooze or scream. That is too bad, for it ranks among the most useful work that economics has produced. The work on how to price financial options turned risk management from a guessing game into a science." *The Economist* (October, 17, 1997).

"Like the titanic, long-term capital management was supposed to be unsinkable. The hedge funds dramatic downfall and bale-out last week was the stuff of Hollywood disaster movies: fortunes laid waste, proud men (Nobel laureates no less) cut down to size, giant tidal waves threatening to drown some of Wall Street's snootiest institutions. At the very least, Wall Street's finest were blinded by the reputation of the LCTM's founders who included Robert Merton and Myron Scholes who last year shared the Nobel Prize for economics for their contributions to the understanding of financial risk." *The Economist* (October, 3, 1998).

"Ola Pehrsson, a Swedish sculptor, has connected a yukka plant to a series of electrodes. These are connected to a computer that is, in turn, connected to share movements on the Swedish stock market. Through its responses to the electrodes and movements on the stock market, the yukka plant tells Ola Pehrsson whether to buy or sell items in his share portfolio. The experiment commenced in January 1999. By the end of December 1999, the yukka plant was outperforming analysts working full-time on the Swedish stock market by 30 per cent." CNN Feature (September, 29, 2000).

Media and other analysts also expect to see certain other calculations. For example:

» headcount and payroll as a percentage of capital value;
» venture investment as a percentage of capital employed;
» overhead as a percentage of capital employed; and
» overhead as a percentage of turnover or gross profit.

Failure to meet these maxima causes concern to analysts; if there are variations from the perceived norms, an explanation is required in advance.

Similarly, profits warnings normally have to be accompanied by very public engagement of top brand consultants and reductions in headcount. These are undertaken in order to preserve short-term stock market values whether or not the actual needs of the business demand them.

One high profile survey of the relationship between UK MNCs and management consultants concluded that this was the over-riding reason for engaging the relationship at all. Another in the USA found no correlation between engaging consultants in business process re-engineering programs and other downsizing activities, and long-term enhanced business performance.

Sources: Banking Federation (UK) (1999) "Corporate Restructuring"; American Management Association (USA) (2000) "The Long-term Effects of Corporate Restructuring."

This is the context in which finance is provided and allocated for the following.

» Product, service, and brand building and the costs of infrastructure, supply, and distribution chains and management information systems to support these.

» Technology and expertise provision in the locations required.

» Marketing, public relations, and organizational and brand awareness programs. Those genuinely seeking long-term and enduringly profitable and effective activities in particular locations spend a large amount of time and resources in becoming broadly familiar with every aspect of the locality, as well as paying attention to the specific business opportunities apparent.

» Product and service mix designs for particular locations. Many MNCs have found that in order to gain market for the core product or service, peripheral activities have had to be engaged in order to gain a foothold. For example, in order to gain markets in Eastern Europe for their main ranges, Volkswagen had first to develop their Skoda brand, which was of Czech origin. In order to gain credence in Malaysia as an expert civil engineering consultant, Ove Arup spent five years getting to know key political figures, work commissioners and large local contractors, with only marginal returns over the period.

This is also the context in which financial reporting takes place. On an annual basis, it is often very difficult to see progress, increases in rates of return or indeed, any payback on work carried out. There is therefore a clear potential conflict between the enduring demands of business development, and the immediacy of the approach of media analysts and stock markets. Those in senior positions in global organizations, who are nevertheless not expert in the truly global aspects of management, consequently find themselves having to choose between short-term stock market value and long-term business advantage.

ORGANIZATION STRUCTURES AND CULTURES

As global organizations and MNCs seek locations for activities in their own preferred areas attention is required to:

» organization structure – the need for rank, division, location, and functional expertise, reporting relationships and communications channels; and

» organization culture – the summary of collective and individual attitudes, values, and beliefs;

The outcome is the ability to "manage diversity" or "manage across cultures." To be effective, this requires acknowledging the differences in attitudes, values, behavior and expectations of those who work in the various locations and activities; and harmonizing talents, qualities, and expertise in accordance with overall policy, strategy, and direction.

Clear standards of attitudes, behavior, and performance have to be established at headquarters and enforced in different locations and circumstances at local and regional levels. Problems arise when there are known, believed or perceived variations, and when organizations take advantage of lack of labor market regulation to impose disadvantageous standards on those in particular locations. A key priority is harmonization between the strengths of the organization and its own distinctive standards, with the age, history, traditions, and social customs of the locality and its patterns of work.

The requirement is a global organization culture that is capable of assimilation anywhere in the world where activities are being considered. It must therefore be:

» strong, not weak;
» unified, not divided;
» designed, not emergent; and
» capable of positive acceptance rather than mere compliance.

This is reinforced by the following.

» Developing and promoting local talent into managerial positions. This is likely to include culture and behavior development, as well as enhancing expertise, because both commitment and capability are required.
» Attracting and retaining local talent so that the bonds between the organization and its localities are reinforced and strengthened. Problems arise when axis management is imposed on localities. The purpose is to develop the whole global organization, as well as the

local operation. Again, this is not always either recognized or valued by senior managers at corporate headquarters.

» Pay levels: which must reflect (if not match) those available elsewhere in the organization, above all those at headquarters (see summary box 6.6).

SUMMARY BOX 6.6: PAY AND VALUE

Levels of pay and reward are a clear indication of the actual value and respect placed on particular activities and staff. The following dimensions require attention.

» The differentials between those at the top and bottom of the organization. The greater the divide, the more coercive and adversarial the structure and culture.

» Racial, gender, national, social, and other ethnic differentials: especially those that must be attended to by law in the EU and USA; and those that need not be attended to elsewhere in the world.

» Differentials between those from the country of origin and indigenous staff on equivalent levels of expertise and responsibility.

» Differentials in other terms and conditions of employment by location and occupation, as well as local or ethnic origin.

Each aspect has either to be capable of sustainable and open support; or else it is necessary to recognize the threat to particular operations when a competitor (especially an MNC) starts to make inroads into the sector or location.

More generally, pay and reward policies reflect the wholesomeness and integrity of organization leadership and management. They give clear perceptions and indications of the broader conduct of business.

Global organizations have the following additional considerations.

» Growth through acquisition, merger, and takeover: overtly straightforward and easily achievable in the short-term; enduring problems are caused if there is no cultural or structural fit (this is the major cause of failure of most mergers and acquisitions).

» Attitudes to local partners, subcontractors, and specialists: the basis on which they are engaged, whether a long-term relationship is envisaged and how the question of dominance-dependence is to be managed (see summary box 6.7).

SUMMARY BOX 6.7: DOMINANCE AND DEPENDENCY

For global organizations, this is a major area of corporate responsibility. By the very nature of their economic size, they are more or less certain to be in the dominant position. The only exception is when they require scarce technology, materials or expertise at short notice.

Global organizations therefore have a clear choice: whether to exploit their position because they can; or whether to accept the responsibility that morally goes with this. For example:

"Labor groups agree that a living wage for an assembly line worker in China would be approximately US 87 cents per hour. In the United States and Germany, where multinationals have closed down hundreds of domestic textile factories to move to Third World production, garment workers are paid an average US $10 and US $18.50 an hour respectively. Yet even with these massive savings in labor costs, those who manufacture for the most prominent and richest brands in the world are still refusing to pay workers in China the 87 cents that would cover the cost of their living, stave off illness and even allow them to send a little money home to their families. A 1998 study of brand name manufacturing in the Chinese special economic zones found that Walmart, Ralph Lauren, Anne Taylor, Esprit, Liz Claiborne, Kmart, Nike, Adidas and others were only paying a fraction of that miserable 87 cents – some were paying as little as 13 cents an hour."

Source: Klein, N. (2001) *No Logo*, Harper Business, London.

» Attention to human resource and labor relations policies and practices: these are led by the extent to which there is a unity of overall corporate attitude towards all staff whatever their location; relationships with trade unions (if any); and whether differential approaches are tolerated, encouraged or actively designed (see summary box 6.6 above). As well as reward levels and terms and conditions of employment, this includes the existence (or not) of quality of working life, work life balance, and occupational health.

» Attention to staff and organization development: the nature and content of induction, orientation, and job training; the extent of opportunities for promotion and development; those to whom these are to be offered; and whether they are to be restricted on an ethnic, gender or locational criteria.

» Attention to specific local issues: including the use of child labor; the use of corporal punishment by local supervisors and managers; length of working hours; whether overtime is compulsory or not; pay and reward levels, the frequency with which these are paid, and stoppages made from their wages.

Effective structure and culture development requires attention to each of these aspects. This, in turn, means that corporate policies are required. These must be based on a full understanding of all of the pressures inherent in each location of activities, and the ability to set standards that transcend them.

ENVIRONMENT MANAGEMENT

Environment management requires addressing the following.

» Laws, rules and regulations imposed by governments, both overall and also for particular sectors, activities, and operations.

» Global concerns about pollution and effluent creation and disposal.

» The effective use of finite resources, taking a corporate view on sustainable development, replenishment, and refurbishment.

Much of this is led by national government, political interests and environmental lobbies. In many cases, it is supported by extensive academic research predicting the consequences of particular courses of action.

Environment management may suffer from the type and quality of political leadership. Over previous decades, unsuccessful attempts were made to get countries such as China and India to adopt perceived environmentally friendly policies in their industrial revolutions. These were resisted on the grounds that to do so, would make their new industries unviable; and politically, this position was perceived to be vindicated when additional support from the West, the World Bank and others was not forthcoming.

Environmental lobbies operate without political or, more importantly, global organization and MNC influence. The onus therefore returns to the organizations themselves to attend to these issues. The key concerns are:

» Regulation compliance: ensuring that standards are adopted that meet local laws and constraints; anticipate local and global trends in general concerns about the environment, how these might be translated into regulations, and what actions will be required of managers as the result; adopt a strategic approach to the environmental impact of all activities and especially the management of waste and effluent. This is likely to require, in the medium to long-term, the development of alternative production and output methods, especially for those activities that depend on fossil fuels for energy, and which use finite, rare or inaccessible materials.

» Recognizing the costs and implications of waste and effluent management and disposal: and understanding that while expedient approaches are likely to be available for some time to come, responsible disposal and maximum recycling will eventually be required.

» Understanding the impact of activities on the environment and the consequences arising: and again, recognizing that replenishment and refurbishment will eventually be required.

Environment management is a key a feature of corporate citizenship and responsibility. No organization likes to be considered bad at managing this part of their business. Those that do take expedient, rather than responsible, approaches and counteract these with extensive public relations campaigns among politicians, the media, and other influential groups in the axis economies. Ultimately, there will only be radical changes in global organization approaches to these issues when it is made in their interests to do so, and when it runs counter to their interest not to do so. This depends on global regulation and enforcement of specific rules, together with trading penalties including restrictions on activities. Because of the extent of global organization influence, the lead for this is going to have to come from the companies themselves.

CONCLUSIONS

Every aspect of management is influenced by the shift in economic power from governments to commercial organizations. In some parts of the world, governments remain able to regulate activities to a greater or lesser extent. Elsewhere, corporate responsibility is required where political influence is not strong enough. This approach is necessary in order to establish a long-term, secure and profitable future, serving the interests of all.

Attention is especially required where organizations are able to use their economic and financial size to influence political processes. This is compounded where the particular government desperately needs commercial inward investment. There are consequently clear and responsible choices required in every aspect of global organization management – strategy, direction, marketing, and finance; and these are certain to become of ever-greater importance as more MNCs achieve truly global coverage and influence.

KEY LEARNING POINTS

All organizations require an understood generic strategic position, and the Porter model (see above) is a clear starting point. For global organizations and MNCs, specific attention is required to:

» a strategic position and approach to each market and location served;

» an understanding and empathy with specific suppliers, customers, clients, and consumers;

» the need for local talent, and its harmonization with overall priorities, direction and expertise;

» the need for local influence, and an understood basis for this in integrity and mutuality of interest;

» the management of strategic, capital, operational and revenue finance across frontiers, and in accordance with the demands of specific activities and markets; and

» the ordering and directing activities in the enduring interest of everyone.

Globalization Success Stories

What makes for successful global organization management? What are the key issues? This chapter offers key insights into both the ability to go global, and also to remain so. It covers three companies – ABB, Nissan, and Mattel – which produce products and services to quality and standard levels that are universally desired and required.

INTRODUCTION

Each of the following case studies offers key insights into both the ability to go global, and also to remain so. The three companies – ABB, Nissan, and Mattel – produce products and services to quality and standard levels that are universally desired and required; and these are supported by service levels, product development and enhancement, and a constant search for improvement in all operational and support areas.

Each has brought its own distinctive approach to become a successful global organization as follows.

» ABB: quality, excellence, and structuring of leadership and direction.
» Nissan: the relationship between excellence in staff management and product and service quality and performance.
» Mattel: sustaining perceived product quality and desirability.

ABB: LEADERSHIP, QUALITY, EXCELLENCE AND STRUCTURE

ABB was formed in 1988 by a merger between ASEA of Sweden and Brown Boveri of Switzerland. The two companies had hitherto been bitter commercial rivals in the engineering, power generation, and capital goods manufacturing industries. At the time, ASEA was looking for overseas acquisitions. Nobody, however, considered that it would wish to merge with its main competitor.

Leadership

Percy Barnevik, the chairman of ASEA, was appointed chief executive officer of the new organization. His strategic approach to business development and globalization was based on seeking opportunities for high added value for the company's products and services, and tailoring these to specific local needs.

The form of leadership for the whole company was designed so that there was a mix of the following.

» Global leaders: developed from among long-serving divisional and functional managers through business schools, rotation and planned service and experience. These members of staff could be brought in from outside or developed from companies as they were taken over.

» Local chieftains (local leaders): Barnevik had set an initial tone for the company that required all local chief executives and general managers to link and act in the best interests of their particular region. There is therefore a high degree of emphasis on local input, market and product research, and client liaison. This is reinforced by employing local nationals in key positions; and in developing them in the ABB expertise and culture. Local leaders may themselves seek opportunities elsewhere within the organization once they have proved themselves capable in their own region.

» Developing the next generation: a key responsibility of corporate headquarters is the selection and development of future generations of managers so that the company does not lose the qualities, expertise, drive and culture that has enabled its growth, success, and profitability of the recent past. Future generations of top managers and global leaders are also required to seek fresh opportunities in new and existing markets and locations, and to organize and direct future market entries and company takeovers.

» Seamless transition: in 1996, Barnevik stepped down as chief executive officer and became company chairman. He was replaced by Goran Lindahl, another ex-ASEA employee. Lindahl had experience in each of the organization's main operating areas. Most important of all, he was the successor chosen by Barnevik himself. At the point of his outgoing, Barnevik structured a new group executive committee to support Lindahl in his new position, and as a pool of global talent, from which the next chief executive would emerge. Jorgen Centermann was appointed head of the automation section at this time. When Lindahl stepped down in January 2001, Centermann was appointed the new chief executive officer. This series of appointments reflects the strong corporate culture – the distinctive ABB way of doing things – and the "design and production" elements of leadership essential in such a situation.

Strategy and structure

ABB built the path to a truly global presence based on the vision of Barnevik (and subsequently Lindahl and Centermann) as follows.

Axis establishment

The initial emphasis was on gaining and consolidating a substantial presence in each of the "axis regions" – Western Europe, North America and the Far East. Already well established in Europe, ABB acquired a more or less instant presence in the USA through the acquisition of Westinghouse Inc. and Combustion Engineering Inc., two large electrical energy, power supply, and generation infrastructure companies.

In the Far East initial acquisitions were made in India, Pakistan, Japan, China, and Taiwan and subsequently in Malaysia, the Philippines, Vietnam, and Thailand.

From each of these key platforms, a localized presence could then be developed, and local chieftains appointed. The drive was to seek opportunities in which ABB could bring its own expertise to bear on local projects, and to develop the local input in ways profitable for the company and beneficial for the particular client or region.

Local knowledge and understanding

A core presence in each of these regions would then be translated into profitable action without reference to headquarters. This meant that local managers had to have the capability to develop local markets, taking advantage of their detailed knowledge and understanding. It also meant that quicker decisions were arrived at on what was viable in terms of the demands of both the company and the locality.

Speed

Barnevik required both speed and quality of decision-making. He set the tone for this by stating that he did not expect 100 per cent of decisions to be right; and nor were there rigid criteria as to how to proceed. Rather, there were guidelines to be followed.

» The ability to use merger opportunities and cost cutting to be a low cost producer.
» The ability to exploit opportunities in niches and services.
» Absolute standards of quality, reliability and service.
» Local markets with entrenched positions.
» Exploitation of financing opportunities.

» Opportunities where competitors are declining and looking to leave markets.
» Staying power for the future.
» Projections as being "the company in power" which can be relied on by local markets in the long-term.
» Strategic capability and flexibility.

Originally produced as a series of guidelines for remaining in the power engineering business, this became the framework for all future activities. Above all, this required both global and local managers to think, analyze, and evaluate opportunities from their own perspective, and arrive at conclusions in terms of their own particular context.

Leadership style

Barnevik's aim was to create a small business atmosphere within a global organization. He stated:

> "ABB are fervent believers in decentralization. When we structure local operations, we always push to create separate legal entities. Separate companies allow you to create real balance sheets with real responsibility for cash flow and dividends. With real balance sheets, managers inherit results from year to year through changes in equity. The separate companies also create more effective tools to recruit and motivate managers and other key staff. People can aspire to meaningful career ladders in companies small enough to understand and be committed to."

Individual operations would therefore be small enough for real identity and positive relationships to be developed. This was then reinforced by the development of "country identity." This re-emphasized both national identity and ABB structure. It enhanced capability for attracting local talent by offering career development across different ABB companies in the same country. It also added to the capability to build and strengthen top-level contact with customers, clients, governments, communities, trade unions, and the media. When the different activities of ABB in a particular country were added together, it would make them a significant local operation rather than a fragmented series of small, specialized operations.

ABB's growth to a position of global influence and presence has been based on a combined approach of acquisitions and takeovers, together with management development and enhancement away from administration, bureaucracy and traditional complex reporting relationships, to dynamism, flexibility, responsibility, local autonomy, and executive authority.

There are three layers of management only: corporate headquarters; local chieftains; and project and operations leaders. This has meant extensive lay-offs in administrative and managerial functions. Starting at the time of the merger between ASEA and Brown Boveri, Barnevik reduced corporate headquarters in all locations, removing convoluted chains and functional offices.

The company reinforced this with the most powerful messages it could find. Rather than calling the process "restructuring" or "delayering," it was referred to as "getting rid of the sandwich people" – i.e. those who were sandwiched between the positions where value was added and positive contributions made.

ABB headquarters has a managerial and administrative staff of 100. Other local offices lost up to 90 per cent of jobs in administrative functions following takeover by ABB. Barnevik, Lindahl, and Centermann all described this as a "war on bureaucracy." This is driven by the need to cut all non-productive expense out of operations and to ensure that the small business atmosphere is created and maintained. Only by doing this could competitive advantage be sustained in the long-term in all areas of activity and local sensitivities be effectively addressed.

Steps to globalization

The long-term enduring success of ABB in maintaining a global presence and supporting this with effective operations is as follows.

» Decentralization to local activities and profit centers.
» Staying close to customers wherever they exist.
» Globalization is primarily concerned with serving local markets better; it is therefore essential to understand that "global" and "local" feed each other.
» Managing across cultures is a practical business need, requiring the gathering of local, national, and international teams.
» Targets must be challenging and demanding.

» Communication is a constant process, the primary purpose of which is to give people a sense of pride and identity.
» Technological competence is essential – both for effective production and service, and also for internal communications.
» A large pool of talent for the future is required, to ensure "seamless transition." The ideal is to have two or three succession candidates ready at all times for every post.
» Organizational and local values must be capable of integration and harmony; and organization values are developed as new local presences are acquired.
» The primary operational drive is practical and results-oriented, rather than theoretical and analytical.
» Long-term enduring shareholder value is the ultimate measurement of performance and effectiveness in a global organization. This requires the capability to manage variations and fluctuations in individual activities.
» The quality and expertise of leadership is paramount.

KEY INSIGHTS

The ABB approach to globalization, and its success, is founded on:
» strategic leadership, with particular reference to the qualities, expertise, background and experience of those in key positions;
» the ability to harmonize organizational demands and priorities with those of clients and local partners in all parts of the world;
» the need for speed in decision-making processes, based on the removal of layers of bureaucracy, chains of command, and extensive procedures;
» attention to cost bases founded on the removal of non-productive functions and activities;
» effective local approaches to management, based on engaging an attitude and culture of "small company familiarity and identity;" and
» leadership and succession, and the "seamless transition" from one chief executive to the next.

Sources: www.ABB.com; www.FT.com; Barham, K. & Heimer, C. (1998) *ABB: The Dancing Giant*, FT Pitman, London; Peters, T. (1994) *Thriving on Chaos*, Macmillan, Basingstoke.

NISSAN: THE RELATIONSHIP BETWEEN STAFF QUALITY AND PRODUCT AND SERVICE EXCELLENCE

The Nissan motor company was founded in Yokohama, Japan in 1902. For the first 60–70 years of its life, it was an indigenous provider, concentrating on supplying transport to the Japanese military, and later developing cars, trucks and vans for commercial and personal use.

In the 1960s, with the domestic market saturated, the company (together with others) turned its attention to overseas markets. Initial analyses established that there were gaps in both quality and volume available in Western Europe, North America, Asia, and Australia. There were also potential markets in South America.

The company began by exporting cars made in Yokohama in the 1960s. Initially, technical quality and reliability were assured; however, it was found that, in many cases, the car bodywork would wear out more quickly than that produced by Western European and North American manufacturers. The company accordingly adopted the following strategic position.

» Extensive local research in target markets.
» Expansion through local manufacture.
» Long-term high, and enduring levels of investment (underwritten by MITI, the Japanese national bank) so that once markets were developed, they could be sustained.

All this was to be built on a distinctive management style, the priorities of which were:

» effective positive staff management; and
» conformist and cooperative labor relations.

Management style and priorities

Style

The company's management style is paternalistic, conformist and open. Corporate decision making is a lengthy process based on the need for extensive consultation at all levels. The Japanese expression for this is *ringi*, which means "binding the roots" – and once the roots are bound, a collective view is assured and progress is then made with the support of all.

This is underwritten at regional and local levels with:

» extensive liaison between headquarters and Yokohama and national and regional offices;
» extensive prescribed local and regional management and supervisory development programs;
» extensive prescribed local and regional staff development programs; and
» a headquarters corporate culture based on high levels of loyalty and commitment and again, reinforced by extensive development of managerial expertise.

Priorities

Strategic and operational priorities are driven by the recognition that distinctive and enduring levels of organizational performance and customer satisfaction are only achieved if the cars are produced to the highest possible levels of quality and performance. This requires targeting markets, product research and development, and a full understanding of what customers would like and what they *will* buy from whom, and under what set of circumstances.

The aim is a fully integrated style, quality, and expertise of management that transcends, rather than adopts, local cultures. When first locating in the UK and USA, the company took the conscious decision to go into areas where there were high structural levels of unemployment following the collapse of primary and secondary traditional industries.

The company also fully understood that there were cultural barriers and prejudices to overcome. Many of those who would either be working for the company or else buying its products, either had their own history of fighting the Japanese from World War II, or else they knew people who had been involved. It was clearly understood at the outset therefore, that nobody would work for a Japanese company if they could avoid it and that nobody would buy Japanese products and services if they could avoid them.

Decisions were taken at headquarters to invest in the USA and UK. Sites were chosen at Smyrna, Tennessee, USA and Washington, Tyne and Wear, UK, areas of high unemployment and social deprivation. The priorities became:

» winning over the local communities;
» undertaking to provide high levels of job and work security; and
» using local sources wherever possible; part of this meant developing local sources from scratch.

The company fully understood that all this would only be achieved if it were put to the test (see summary box 7.1).

SUMMARY BOX 7.1: RESISTANCE TO NISSAN

Resistance to Nissan in setting up manufacturing operations in the West took the following forms.

» Political: on the grounds that profits would be returned to Japan rather than reinvested in the West.
» Industrial: on the grounds that it would "transform" the nature of the automobile manufacturing and distribution industry, and pricing policies. There were especial concerns about product flooding and dumping.
» Labor relations: on the grounds that these would be "screw-driver assembly" operations, rather than true manufacturing, since all the cars would be brought in kit form from Japan. This was true at first – there was no manufacturing capability in the West until developed by the company.

None of these came to pass. Profits were returned to headquarters, but this was accompanied by high levels of investment that continue to the present. Nissan and other Japanese car and electrical goods companies had never had to use their unit cost advantage to engage in price wars. In many locations, the company charges the highest levels of price for particular product ranges.

Those resisting on the grounds of labor relations have had their protests drowned out by the rush for what turned out to be well paid, rewarding and, compared to the past, much more secure jobs. The cooperative and conformist approach to labor relations was found also to be much less stressful than the adversarial management style adopted by the industries that previously operated in the locations.

Labor relations

The structure on which labor relations is built is as follows.

Partnership and consultation

Partnership is where the company, staff and any recognized trade union acknowledge that all their interests are best served through the creation and development of long-term success and profitable activities.

Consultation includes openness, completeness, and access of information to all. Consultation takes place on specific issues:

» productivity levels and rates;
» quality of working life and environment;
» staff training and development;
» immediate and future business prospects; and
» financial performance and productivity outputs.

The operations in Western Europe are supported by the establishment of works councils, as required by EU law. The view is adopted that this is an additional strand in the creation of fully integrated staff management. Specific directives issued from headquarters in Japan are made available to everyone. Anyone may gain access to managerial staff to seek information or clarification on any issue at all.

Trade union recognition

The company undertakes to work with a single union acting as the staff representative body. The single union approach is seen as beneficial because from the company's point of view, there is no need to manage the differences between the aims and objectives of different representative bodies. There is a history of adversarial, confrontational and ultimately, destructive and expensive labor relations in many multi-union industries and sectors in the West. A much better mutual understanding is built if there are just the two parties.

From the staff point of view, there might be some initial resistance if they do not immediately see any professional, occupational or personal affinity between themselves and the particular union. This was a real management problem when Nissan first established in the UK, because most local unions had been founded either for specific industries (e.g. National Union of Mineworkers) or specific occupations (e.g. nursing and teaching). The trade union chosen in the UK was the Amalgamated Electrical and Engineering Union (AEEU); while this was acceptable to those engaged in manufacture, the union had no history of representing clerical, administrative, sales, and marketing grades.

Elsewhere the company has created its own internal union or staff association, which is given independent support by the company so that it can act with full autonomy on behalf of the staff and particular location. Whichever approach is adopted, there is a key responsibility on the part of unions and staff representatives to market themselves to all staff and demonstrate particular capability in the situation.

Disputes management

Disputes management involves the emphasis being placed on "positive avoidance." Managers and supervisors are extensively trained in staff management policies and practices. They are expected to resolve disputes at the point at which they arise. Formal procedures exist at all locations. These are a combination of guidelines issued from headquarters, and application according to specific regulations and local "best practice."

When disputes and grievances do arise, the requirement is that they are settled to the satisfaction of all. Failure to do so leads to binding pendulum arbitration in which, at the ultimate point of "no resolution," an arbitrator agreed by both sides is appointed. The arbitrator hears the case and then decides *solely* in favor of *one* party without compromise. One party therefore wins; the other loses. There is a serious social, cultural, professional, and occupational stigma placed on managers who lose disputes.

Pay and rewards

The company undertakes to pay at or near the top of the going rate for the particular industry and location. Thus for example, Nissan staff in the UK receive salaries about one quarter higher than those offered by Ford UK and GM Vauxhall. Staff in the USA receive salaries equivalent to those paid in Detroit, but they have much greater degrees of job security, organization and staff consultation, and opportunities for personal, professional, and occupational development.

Training and development

All staff are required to undertake 20–30 days training and development per annum. This is related to present and future demands. Those working on car production are trained in all manufacturing operations so that they can be relocated and rotated between activities. They are also trained in product, service, and personal development so that they can assume responsibility for accepting and managing customer complaints, quality assurance, and overall excellence.

Management and supervisory development concentrates on problem solving. This is reinforced by the need to concentrate on organizational, operational, and staff priorities, rather than the operation of procedures. Managers and supervisors are expected to be visible and accessible at all times.

Management development is a joint responsibility. Managers are expected to appraise their own performance and identify gaps and opportunities. Those in non-managerial positions are given opportunities for promotion, variety, and enhancement; and development programs are worked out between individuals and their supervisor.

At the point of setting up, Nissan spent an average of $16,000 per member of staff on initial and continuing job training and development. Current expenditure is of the order of $10,000 per member of staff per annum on training and development; this attends to all areas of production and service provision, as well as technical, occupational, and professional development.

Productivity

Nissan's productivity rate is approximately 90 cars per member of staff per annum worldwide. The factory at Washington, Tyne and Wear,

UK produces 111 cars per member of staff per annum. Overall, the company's productivity rate is the highest in the world and far in excess of indigenous European and North American producers (e.g. Peugeot, Volkswagen, Citroen, Renault, and Fiat all operate at approximately 50 cars per member of staff per annum; Ford and General Motors at approximately 60 cars per member of staff per annum).

Nissan's competitive advantage stems from these high levels of productivity and these can only be sustained through the development of fully flexible working. As well as the training and development effort, all staff are placed on "salary plus overtime," and may be required to work as and where directed. The expectation is that within three months of commencing employment, all staff are able to carry out all tasks in their particular sphere of work; and they must be prepared to do so if required or requested.

Staff are also required to accept personal and occupational responsibility and accountability for finished product quality, and to handle complaints if these arise. There are no separate quality assurance functions. Queries and complaints from customers are referred to the particular production crew.

Responsibility for executive decision making, product schedules, and quotas and problem solving rests with local supervision and general management. In particular, managers are expected to sort out supply, production, and distribution issues where they occur, and to take active steps to anticipate and resolve them. Managerial expertise in all areas places staff at the core, and the effective resolution of all issues depends on staff capability.

The intended outcome of full flexibility and continuous development combines operational effectiveness and excellence with job security and protection. Nissan's original commitment was to "a lifetime guarantee of employment." In practice, this has turned out not to be possible in all circumstances, though to date, the company has avoided compulsory lay-offs in Western Europe. During one crisis in which the market declined and there was serious over-production, the company offered voluntary severance to those staff that wished to take it, though this was not followed up with temporary lay-offs or compulsory redundancies. During a further crisis, the company engaged in a program of full consultation with all staff as to how the situation might best be managed. The result was that the company created internal staff management and working groups to address problems that were hitherto being attended to by external expertise, business and management consultants, and marketing contractors.

Conclusions

Staff management at Nissan has the core purpose of gaining, maintaining, and developing loyalty and mutual commitment. It enhances attitudes of flexibility and responsiveness, customer and client satisfaction, and product and market development.

The company recognizes that ultimate responsibility for continuing to deliver this lies with management. Having set high and distinctive standards, the company must deliver its part of the agreement. The keys to this are openness and access to information; high levels of pay, reward, and job security; and continued attention to training and development.

If the company fails to deliver any of these elements, then the whole edifice crumbles. In particular, in the locations chosen outside Japan, there is a long history of adversarial labor relations; and if Nissan were to fail to continue to deliver this level of responsibility, the company would very quickly lose its reputation and become "just another employer."

KEY INSIGHTS

Nissan's success in becoming a global organization is based primarily on the effectiveness of staff management. A direct relationship is drawn between staff capability and willingness, and enduring profitability, product quality, and customer and client satisfaction. This expertise in staff management has the following key elements:

» strategic decision-making based on consultation, the ultimate aim of which is universal agreement and understanding;

» the contribution of junior management and supervision in maintaining and developing effective labor relations and employee capability;

> » the levels of investment necessary to develop this expertise;
> » managerial obligations in setting and ensuring absolute standards of staff management, behavior and performance; and
> » the need for effective engagement with trade unions, other representative bodies and staff management associations.
>
> **Sources**: www.nissanmotors.com; Wickens, P. (1993) *The Road to Nissan*, Macmillan, Basingstoke; Wickens, P. (1998) *The Ascendant Organization*, Macmillan, Basingstoke.

MATTEL: ENDURING PERCEIVED PRODUCT QUALITY AND DEVELOPMENT

Mattel Inc. was founded in 1945 in Los Angeles. Originally it produced picture frames, musical instruments, and then diversified into children's toys: initially replica guns and holsters inspired by cinema and TV westerns.

Transformation

In 1959, Mattel introduced Barbie. The first Barbie doll sported black hair, a ponytail hairstyle, a black and white striped bathing suit, open-toed shoes, sunglasses, and earrings. A line of fashions and accessories was subsequently made available. Both little girls and their mothers (those who used the product and those who bought it) took to it immediately and the company was swamped with orders.

The Barbie doll was introduced as a teenage fashion model. She has subsequently taken on many aspiration type roles including: dentist; doctor; firefighter; astronaut; racing driver; show-jumper; and sports car enthusiast.

Development

Over the years, both the company and the product have developed as follows.

> » Barbie's family: this includes her boyfriend Ken, sisters and friends such as Midge, Skipper, and Christie; baby sister Kelly; and baby sister Chrissy. She has also had a number of friends from a wide range of

ethnic backgrounds. A disabled friend in a wheelchair, Becky, was introduced in 1997.

» Barbie is sold in 160 countries around the world. Mattel has developed the product by making local product lines and fashions available in different countries according to taste and need; and acquiring local toy and games manufacturers to achieve mutual advantage and "synergy." This contributes both to local and universal brand, product, and company development.

» Mattel has acquired the rights to specific children's fashions, fads, and interests that can be developed using the Barbie image and appearance. For example, the company has acquired the rights to Pokahontas, The Lion King, and Aladdin; while the products are differentiated by packaging, the clothes and accessories are universally interchangeable with the core Barbie offering.

In the 1980s, the company divested itself of all non-toy related activities. It began the strategy that continues to the present: maximizing core brands, while at the same time identifying new brands with core potential. This has been achieved through:

» entering licensing arrangements with major children's entertainers, including the Walt Disney Company, J.K. Rowling and Harry Potter, and Nickelodeon; and

» acquiring key players in the toys sector: in 1993, the company took over Fisher-Price and the Learning Company Inc., a top maker of software products. The Learning Company Inc. was subsequently sold on; however, Mattel used its experience in this to develop its own Website provision enabling both children and their parents to download product information and new ideas from the company.

Manufacturing

Some of the company's products are made in the West, especially England, France, Germany, South Africa, and Italy. The overwhelming volume of the core product is manufactured in Mexico and the People's Republic of China. In support of this the company has developed a monitoring body, the Mattel Independent Monitoring Council (MIMCO). MIMCO undertakes regular inspections of all manufacturing facilities. The company is committed to taking remedial action where those working in the factories are found to be working under unacceptable or oppressive conditions. Mattel describes itself as: "The first global consumer products company to apply this system to its facilities and core contractors on a worldwide basis."

In particular, the company uses two factories in China: Guan Yao and Chang An. These have regularly given cause for concern. MIMCO concentrated on: the number of hours being worked by members of staff; the quality of air in manufacturing plants; pay and reward levels; quality of meals; and the living conditions in the dormitories in which those who work in the factories live.

Specific problems were found with the length of hours being worked; the presence of paint and plastic fumes in the factories; and low levels of wages. The company gave the factories an initial six months to make improvements. An interim inspection in November 2000 concluded that some progress had been made; and MIMCO inspectors undertook to return the following year. The key requirements are the following.

» Continued attention to cleanliness and safety in the working environment.
» Regular medical check-ups; and mandatory medical check-ups at the time of employment.
» Lavatory facilities, drinking water and other amenities must meet the applicable country laws and Mattel's own global manufacturing principles.
» New employees are furnished with written copies of employment agreements.
» There must be no employees under the age of 16.
» All new employees must be given initial and continuing job training activities; and also offered non-job related skill enhancement programs and general education.
» Employees must be offered the opportunity to participate in union related and other types of labor relations activities.

Conclusions

Mattel Inc. has effectively identified and managed a number of key conditions over a long period of time as a critical element of its enduring success. These are:

» the constant development of Barbie, the core brand, and the capability to ensure that this remains acceptable and desirable in each market served;

» the integration of the core with local offerings (the Walt Disney tie-ins, USA; JW Spears, UK); and

» continued attention to product differentiation and service development, in order to keep everything fresh and current so that customers remain loyal and active purchasers.

The company has taken active steps towards discharging the broad range of responsibilities inherent in global activities. While much remains to be done on the employment practice side, the company is committed to improving all aspects of its activities as a condition of ensuring its long-term future profitability.

KEY INSIGHTS

The primary lesson from Mattel is the need to have a core product that can be made both universally acceptable and developed in ways of specific interest to particular markets. The company concentrates on the core, and seeks peripheral opportunities in specific locations only when these can be developed in harmony with the core, and not at its expense. The company has also developed its business through:

» licensing and acquisition, again where these support the core rather than dilute it;

» attention to the supply side, to ensure both product and packaging quality; and

» active social and ethical responsibility, especially in terms of employment practice in its Third World suppliers.

Key Concepts and Thinkers

This chapter provides a global organization glossary and also details related key concepts and thinkers.

GLOSSARY

Alienation – Feelings of being helpless and powerless in particular situations; above all, applying to those working without influence in their organization; and those working in remote locations without influence over the organization as a whole.

Axis economies – "The axis" is identified as Western Europe, the United States of America and Japan: the main areas of the world in states of advanced economic development.

Barriers – Entry barriers are those that either preclude organizations from entering sectors or localities, or those which have to be cleared as a consequence of wishing to enter particular sectors or localities. Exit barriers are those that have to be cleared as the result of decisions taken to withdraw from particular activities or locations; a key exit barrier is the loss of reputation and adverse media coverage that may occur as the result of a decision to withdraw.

Cartel – A system of price fixing and agreement entered into by organizations in particular sectors or localities.

Cold War – The state of armed hostility (but not open conflict) that existed between "the West" led by the USA and NATO countries, and the USSR and Warsaw Pact countries, between 1948–1990.

Compliance – The physical and psychological state of being that exists when a person or group agrees to work for an organization under a specific set of conditions.

Economies of scale – Factors that cause the average cost of producing something to drop as output is increased, the savings that can be made by manufacturing goods or supplying services in large quantities.

Economies of scope – The savings that can be made by producing a broad range of goods or services, either as core offerings, or in which the core product or service is related to localized offerings.

Federations – Forms of organization that engage in long-term supply, production, distribution, and service relationships; the organizations retain an overt measure of independence, though, in practice, they are likely to be more or less mutually dependent.

Individualized corporations - A model of global organizations based on the contribution of individual expertise to continued success (see also Ghoshal and Bartlett, Chapter 9).

Marketing mixes - Combinations of product and service presentation and content based on product, price, place, and promotion; customers, convenience, choice, and content.

Multinational corporations (MNCs) - Any organization that trades or locates in places other than its country of domicile or origin.

NATO - The North Atlantic Treaty Organization.

Networks - Formal and informal arrangements between individuals, groups and organizations aimed at developing business performance and individual and collective expertise.

Return on investment - The financial and other returns desired, and required, as the result of engaging in particular activities.

Risk - The relationship between what is known and can be predicted, what is understood and might be predicted, and what is unknown and cannot be predicted, in particular activities.

Synergies - "The whole is greater than the sum of its parts"; the key driver in the process of globalization by merger and acquisition.

Stakeholders - Anyone who has an interest in the performance of an organization; the key stakeholders are: staff, backers, the financial interest, suppliers, customers and clients, and communities.

Switching costs - The costs incurred by organizations in switching from one set of activities, or one location, to another.

Transnational corporations - Those that operate across international boundaries.

United Nations - The federated arrangement of countries and governments created in 1946.

United Nations Children's Foundation (UNICEF) - The United Nations body responsible for the global welfare of children.

United Nations High Commission on Refugees (UNHCR) - The United Nations commission responsible for the welfare of refugees and displaced persons.

World Trade Organization - The trans-governmental body established to regulate global trading practices.

World Bank - The trans-governmental organization created to provide finance and investment where it would otherwise not be available.

Works councils – Statutory bodies required by all organizations operating within the European Union (EU); at present, this is limited to all
organizations with 20 or more staff, though it is expected to extend
to all organizations, whatever their size, in the future.

RELATED CONCEPTS AND THINKERS

Scientific management

The concept of scientific management was pioneered by F.W. Taylor
(1856-1917), and he also put his own ideas into practice. The overall
approach was founded in the need to be as precise as possible about the
problems of work and work organization. It was based on the premise
that proper organization of the workforce and work methods would
improve efficiency. Work should be a cooperative effort between
management and workers. Work organization should be such that
it removed all responsibility from the workers, leaving them only
with their particular task. By specializing and training in this task,
the individual worker would become perfect in job performance.
Work could therefore be organized into production lines and items
produced efficiently and to a constant standard as the result. Precise
performance standards would be predetermined by job observation
and analysis and a best method arrived at; this would then become the
normal way of working. Everyone would benefit – the organization,
because it had cut out all wasteful and inefficient use of resources;
managers, because they had a known standard of work to set and
observe; and workers, because they would always do the job in the
same way.

Everyone would benefit financially also from the increase in output,
sales, and profits, and this would be reflected in high wage and salary
levels. The approach was developed by F.W. Taylor from a research
point of view, and incorporated by Ford as the key to manufacturing
success, output, and efficiency. This work foreshadowed production
line and other standardized and automated efforts and techniques that
have been used for mass produced goods and commodities ever since.

Scientific management also helped to create boredom, disaffection,
and alienation of the workforces that produced these goods; these still
remain key managerial issues to be addressed and resolved at present.

Sources: Taylor, F.W. (1947) *Scientific Management*, Harper & Row, New York; Luthans, F. (1996) *Organizational Behavior*, McGraw Hill, New York.

Cultures' consequences

The relationship between culture and performance in global organizations was established by Geert Hofstede, who carried out in-depth work, attitude, behavior, and performance surveys among the 116,000 staff of IBM in 40 countries. He identified basic dimensions of national cultural factors, and the differences in their emphases and importance in various countries. The four dimensions were as follows.

» *Power-distance* – the extent to which power and influence is distributed across the society; the extent to which this is acceptable to the members of the society; access to sources of power and influence; and the physical and psychological distance that exists between people and the sources of power and influence.
» *Uncertainty-avoidance* – the extent to which people prefer order and certainty, or uncertainty and ambiguity; and the extent to which they feel comfortable or threatened by the presence or absence of each.
» *Individualism-collectivism* – the extent to which individuals are expected, or expect, to take care of themselves; the extent to which a common good is perceived and the tendency and willingness to work towards this.
» *Masculinity-femininity* – the distinction between masculine values (the acquisition of money, wealth, fortune, success, ambition, possessions) and the feminine (sensitivity, care, concern, attention to the needs of others, quality of life); and the value, importance, mix, and prevalence of each in different areas.

Sources: Hofstede, G. (1980) *Cultures' Consequences*, Sage, London; Hofstede, G. (1992) *Cultures and Organizations*, Harper Collins Business, London.

Excellence

The genesis of the work that subsequently became known as the ''excellence studies'' was a review carried out during the 1970s by McKinsey

& Co., the international management consulting firm, of its thinking and approach to business strategy and organizational effectiveness.

The approach adopted was to study organizations and managers of high reputation and/or performance, and to try and isolate those qualities and characteristics that make them so. In all, 62 organizations were studied. These were drawn from all sectors of US industry and commerce, and included many global firms (e.g. Boeing, McDonald's, Hewlett Packard, 3M).

High performing addressed:

» profitability;
» globalization and global influence;
» strong positive images and reputation;
» strength of performance, whether in domestic markets, slumped or declining markets, or growing and expanding markets;
» customer and client confidence; and
» staff and customer loyalty.

The studies identified eight characteristics of excellent managerial and organizational practice as follows.

» *Bias for action* – do it, fix it, try it.
» *Closeness to the customer* – listening intently and regularly to customer needs and wants and providing quality, service, and reliability.
» *Autonomy and entrepreneurship* – innovation and risk taking as an expected way of doing things, rather than conformity and conservatism.
» *Productivity through people* – in which employees are placed at the core of organizational excellence and profitability.
» *Hands on, value drive* – the basic philosophy of the organization is well defined and understood.
» *Stick to the knitting* – concentrating on what you can do well.
» *Simple form, lean staff* – concentrating staff efforts at the frontline, and keeping systems and procedures simple, with small amounts of headquarters staff.
» *Simultaneous loose-tight properties* – centralized control of values with operational decentralization and autonomy.

The effectiveness of each of these elements depended on the following foundations.

» *Organization culture* – the need to reflect the belief in being the best; a belief in the importance of the staff; a belief in, and obsession with, quality and service; a belief that organization members should innovate and have their creative capacities harnessed and rewarded; and a belief in the importance of excellent communication among all staff.

» *Macro-organizational analysis* – dependent upon the strength and style of leadership: the drive, determination, core values, and strategic vision necessary to energize and make profitable the organization's activities. This is reinforced by a belief in continuous development, and recognition that there is always room for improvement in both products and services, and also management and organizational processes.

Sources: Peters, T. & Waterman, R.H. (1980) *In Search of Excellence*, Harper & Row, New York; Peters, T. & Austin, N. (1986) *A Passion for Excellence: The Leadership Difference*, Harper & Row, New York; Peters, T. (1990) *Thriving on Chaos*, Macmillan, Basingstoke; Kanter, R.M. (1985) *When Giants Learn to Dance*, Free Press, New York; Kanter, R.M. (1990) *The Change Masters*, Free Press, New York.

The global business and global management principles

The need to establish the core elements of successful business globalization and a set of management principles to support this was the driving force of work carried out by Ronnie Lessem in the 1980s. Lessem, a Zimbabwean academic, had previously worked in retail distribution, supermarket management, and the supply side. He identified a combination of guts, brains, heart, and soul necessary to be a successful and effective global operator. These are traced through a combination of the following.

» Economic development with roots in the first Industrial Revolution of the eighteenth and nineteenth centuries in which entrepreneurial attributes were required as follows:

» the capacity to work hard;
» enthusiasm and the ability to arouse it in others;
» mental agility;
» will, persistence, and emotional resilience;
» capacity to improvise, as well as to organize; and
» imagination, hunch and instinct.
» Management development in which corporations required professional staff to run them with "brains" – capability, willingness, and distinctive expertise, as well as guts as follows:
  » productivity;
  » effective teamwork;
  » coordination and control;
  » strategic and operational capability;
  » formal and informal organization;
  » marketing; and
  » innovation.
» Total development, the outcome of which is the integration of design, technology, people, and enterprise.
» Transcendence, in which activities and behavior come to depend on the collective heart and soul of the organization and the capability and expertise of those who work for it.

Within this, four groups of heroes are identified.

» *Heroes of the west* – intrapreneurs, enterprising individuals acting within established organizations to develop and enhance both their individual capability and organizational performance.
» *Heroes of the north* – managers of change and change agents, encouraging and implementing fresh activities in all aspects of organizational performance, and seeking global, as well as local, advantages.
» *Heroes of the east* – corporate architects responsible for producing organizational formats able to serve customers and develop business based on the expertise with which they are designed and managed.
» *Heroes of the south* – visionaries, responsible for accepting, understanding, considering, and bringing about the wider social and ethical contributions and benefits that effective business inherently develops.

The work draws on global organizations from a range of sectors.

» Sony, responsible for setting the prevailing standards of electrical goods, music, and video entertainment worldwide.
» Zerox, responsible for setting the global standard for document reproduction, presentation, and delivery, both in volume and quality terms.
» 3M, which transformed from mining and quarrying into the world's leading stationery and office supplies company.

The different threads are then drawn together. This is summarized as "living business," reflecting the critical nature of the human involvement at each stage – and the consequent responsibilities to "humanity."

Sources: Lessem, R.S. (1986) *The Global Business*, Prentice Hall International, New Jersey; Lessem, R.S. (1989) *Global Management Principles*, Prentice Hall International, New Jersey; Lessem, R.S. (1992) *Transforming Management*, Prentice Hall International, New Jersey.

Resources

Much has been written about global organizations. This chapter identifies the major contributions to the overall understanding of the opportunities, expertise, and responsibilities inherent in global business and the management of global organizations.

INTRODUCTION

Each of the resources indicated below makes a major contribution to the overall understanding of the opportunities, expertise, and responsibilities inherent in global business and the management of global organizations. These are:

» market assessment and management;
» organizational, operational, and market responsibilities;
» the complexities of global business and management;
» the forms of organization; and
» the need for strategy and direction.

CLARK, E. (1988) *THE WANT MAKERS*, CORGI, LONDON

Produced twelve years before the end of the twentieth century, this work identifies almost for the first time, a truly global perspective on markets and marketing. As well as identifying global markets, Clark analyzes approaches that were beginning to be undertaken by the then very much smaller global players.

The global markets identified are:

» tobacco;
» alcohol;
» drugs and pharmaceuticals;
» cosmetics;
» children; and
» politics.

Early entrants into global fields adopted the view that successful marketing brand and product development was achieved as the result of targeted promotion, public relations, lobbying, and media coverage. If this could be reinforced with product placement, sponsorship, and overtly philanthropic acts, so much the better.

Once entry and awareness had been achieved, organizations could then make major efforts at targeting individuals and groups critical to wider brand acceptance and purchase. Accordingly, for example:

» UK doctors were targeted with public relations expenditure by pharmaceutical companies of $5,000 per individual doctor in the

1980s (the present figure is $14,000). This was (and is) directed at getting doctors to prescribe particular branded drugs, antibiotics, and other products for which premium prices could then be charged back to the UK National Health Service and public and private medical insurance organizations.

» Globally, tobacco companies targeted their efforts at sports sponsorship. Once, this included sponsorship of the women's tennis tour (Virginia Slims). Subsequent efforts helped enable extensive coverage of rugby league, soccer, all motor sports, as well as indoor events such as snooker, darts, and pool. At present, tobacco sponsorship is the largest single financier of Formula One grand prix motor racing ($237 million per annum).

» Children could be sold anything provided that "fun, clean, and wholesome images" were produced, and provided that parents were prepared to pay. This has subsequently been a key feature of brand development in garments and mobile phones. It continues as a core element of advertising and marketing campaigns of those products studied at the time by Clark (McDonald's, Barbie, Nike, and Reebok).

» Politics could be made to look effective provided that sufficient attention was paid to the ways in which particular messages were delivered. While these lessons had been learned piecemeal in the past (e.g. by Hitler and the Kennedys), they had not so far been codified, nor universally understood. It was now possible, however, to package and brand politics in exactly the same way as other commodities.

KLEIN, N. (2001) *NO LOGO*, HARPER COLLINS, LONDON

This work is the product of four years' extensive research and investigation. The result is a highly detailed and fully supported treatise on the darker side of global organizations, above all, those that use their financial size and dominant position to impose:

» the burden of cost cutting and margin advantage on third world suppliers;

» product and service quality, standards, and price ranges on customers through the operation of cartel-type arrangements in the markets served; and
» terms and conditions of employment and wage levels of third world producers and subcontractors.

The thesis of targeting, developing, and dominating universal markets (see Clark above) is then pursued, but from the point of view of:

» the relationships between politicians and corporations;
» children and youth markets;
» branded school and university education;
» market flooding and dumping by oil, chemical, garment, soft drinks, fast food, automobile, and hi-tech producers and retailers; and
» the relationship between products, services, and lifestyles ("the marketing of 'cool'").

The final part of the work studies the limitation of the influence and activities of global organizations. It then goes on to document some of the actions taken by protest groups and others concerned at the ways in which global organizations and MNCs are using their influence in setting social, political, and cultural agenda and norms, rather than concentrating on economic activities and operations. These actions, while of limited universal effect, have raised concerns around:

» the position of the global organization as the eliminator, rather than the provider, of choice;
» price levels and marketing ethics;
» wider social and economic responsibilities; and
» management of the development of the Third World in everyone's interests, rather than purely as a channel of assured income for global organizations.

Moreover, arguments are being developed from a point of view of informed, as well as emotional, response; the knowledge-base of those seeking alternatives is therefore as great as that present in the global organizations, even if the influence is not (see Fig 9.1).

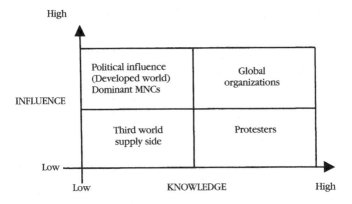

High

INFLUENCE

| Political influence (Developed world) Dominant MNCs | Global organizations |
| Third world supply side | Protesters |

Low

Low · KNOWLEDGE · High

Fig. 9.1 The Knowledge-Influence Spectrum. (Source: Pettinger, R. (2000) *Investment Appraisal: A Managerial Approach*, Macmillan, Basingstoke.).

GHOSHAL, S. & BARTLETT, C. (1990) *MANAGING ACROSS BORDERS*; AND (1998) *THE INDIVIDUALIZED CORPORATION*, BUTTERWORTH HEINEMANN, OXFORD

Ghoshal and Bartlett identify approaches to globalization based on the following.

» *Global strategies* – based on organization-based standards of policy, direction and management that ensure delivery of products and services that will be of acceptable quality and value everywhere that they are made available.
» *Multinational strategies* – in which policy and direction are differentiated by location in order to take advantage of local trading conditions, technological availability, and the prosperity levels of markets.
» *International strategies* – based on the ability to produce products and services to the standards required by specific locations and to set price levels accordingly. For example, hotel rooms of universal basic standard are required by Western travelers but cannot be priced at the same level in up-country Vietnam as those available in central London. Cars produced for African and Eastern European markets do

not have to meet the same exhaust pollution criteria as those on sale in the EU. This is supported by:

» the outdated concept of bureaucracy, rank, and hierarchy as a core form of corporate governance;

» the need for local and regional autonomy together with strategic, not operational, reporting relationships between activities and headquarters;

» the need to develop high levels of knowledge and expertise in managers and other key figures.

The result of this is capability and effectiveness in strategy and policy implementation, and the resolution of technical operating and labor relations problems.

The foundation for success is transmitted from organization structure to individual excellence. This is based on high and continued levels of education, development, variety and experience, and qualities of collective and corporate, as well as individual flexibility, responsiveness, creativity, and ingenuity. Everything can then be directed at customer and market service in terms that satisfy everyone rather than being limited and constrained by policies and systems.

The shift is achieved by concentrating on organizational and managerial philosophies based on:

» securing and rewarding individual excellence;

» direct relationships between strategy and purpose related to corporate demands and the precise reasons for being in particular locations;

» organizational processes that support, rather than direct, the frontline;

» individualized autonomy for those in the frontline, as well as middle and corporate positions, thus enabling the pursuit of broad and agreed remits according to the demands of the particular situation in ways that appear the best to those present, rather than those at headquarters. Managers at all levels therefore become supporters and enablers, rather than drivers and prescribers.

HAMEL, G. (2001) *LEADING THE REVOLUTION, HARVARD BUSINESS SCHOOL PRESS, BOSTON*

Hamel takes the view that corporate structures, anticipated financial returns and stock market performance act as brakes, rather than drives, for product and service effectiveness. The elements required in global organizations are the following.

Managing risk

Managing risk by taking the risk out of particular ventures and activities through processes of analysis, education, information management, training, and development. This must be extended to include customers, clients, suppliers, media, and financial analysts, as well as stockholders and financial interests. In this way, the risk of operating in particular spheres is reduced because the ground rules are known and understood in advance. Those involved therefore know and understand the opportunities, constraints, and obligations that consequently accrue. Rather than acknowledging that things might go wrong, the outcome is a full understanding of the total situation so that both the number, and also the critical nature of pitfalls are kept to a minimum and can be avoided wherever possible.

Gray-haired revolutionaries

Gray-haired revolutionaries: the term is used to emphasize the fact that long-established (gray-haired) organizations and their top managers require new approaches, not just start-ups and the new breed of company. Gray-haired revolutionary managers and companies have the dual capacity of reinventing their core strategies and contributing to industry-wide revolution. The key elements are:

» outrageously ambitious growth objectives that are unattainable without innovation;
» working from the customer inward rather than from existing processes outward;
» innovative meritocracy, the outcome of which is the reward of excellence, creativity, and expertise;
» rapid experimentation and prototyping so that ideas can be tested and developed; or else that failure becomes apparent at a very early stage;
» loose and evolving definitions of product and service offerings to avoid being boxed in by organizational perceptions; and
» recognizing outside influences and accepting lessons from elsewhere when they can be clearly made to be of value.

The management of portfolios

These are:

» portfolios of experiments, some of which will work and others will not; all serve as a basis for corporate, collective, and individual learning and development;

» portfolios of qualities, required of all visionary and revolutionary companies whatever their age, and including flexibility, dynamism, responsiveness, enthusiasm, commitment, and locality management;

» portfolios of ventures, so that the whole is developed as each of the parts (ventures) come to fruition;

» portfolios of partners, whereby all organizations, from time to time, need expertise, technology, sources, and subcontractors. These are only effectively led and managed if they are respected and valued as partners rather than seen purely as resources to be exploited.

PORTER, M.E. (1980) *COMPETITIVE STRATEGY: TECHNIQUES FOR ANALYZING INDUSTRIES AND COMPETITORS,* FREE PRESS, NEW YORK

Porter's contribution to the effective development of global organizations is:

» emphasizing the need for strategic approaches based on market identification and sustainable resource allocation;

» recognizing that all markets are ultimately competitive and that the degree, as well as the fact of rivalry must be assessed;

» recognizing that if one organization sees an advantage in a particular location, others will do so also; and

» the need for analyzing all aspects of the competitive position and environment.

The key approaches are as follows.

Five forces

A five forces model can be seen in Fig 9.2.

For global organizations, the keys are:

» assessing the supply and distribution elements from the point of view of ensuring that sufficient volumes of each are available;

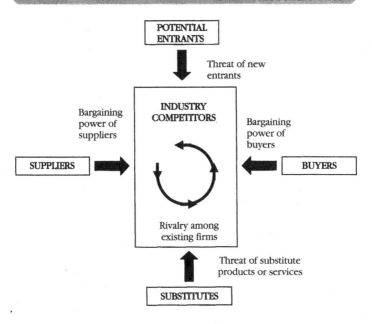

Fig. 9.2 Five Forces Model.

and designing and managing the logistics on the scope and scale necessary;

» considering the threat of entry from the broadest possible point of view, including the prospect of taking over potential entrants and substitutes; and

» understanding the consequences of changes in degrees of rivalry; and the sudden entry or withdrawal of another key player.

Competitor analysis

The components of a competitor analysis can be seen in Fig 9.3.

The key point of inquiry is "assumptions." The sheer size of global organizations means that assumptions tend to be taken as read rather than tested and evaluated. Questioning assumptions must arrive at

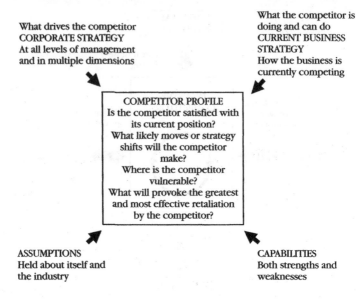

What drives the competitor
CORPORATE STRATEGY
At all levels of management
and in multiple dimensions

What the competitor is
doing and can do
CURRENT BUSINESS
STRATEGY
How the business is
currently competing

COMPETITOR PROFILE
Is the competitor satisfied with
its current position?
What likely moves or strategy
shifts will the competitor
make?
Where is the competitor
vulnerable?
What will provoke the greatest
and most effective retaliation
by the competitor?

ASSUMPTIONS
Held about itself and
the industry

CAPABILITIES
Both strengths and
weaknesses

Fig. 9.3 The Components of a Competitor Analysis.

genuine evaluation of what competitors can, and cannot, do. Because competitors have not done something in the past, this does not preclude them from doing so in the future.

Industry analyses require different emphases depending on whether they are:

» emergent, in which case strategy is developed along lines of "informed assumption;"
» fragmented, in which case organizations play to their individual strengths;
» mature, in which case industries are open to fresh and new approaches based on innovation, design, branding, and differentiation; or
» declining, in which case organizations need to plan for whether or not they are going to stay in the sector; if so, how to operate profitably; if not, how to withdraw without loss of wider reputation.

The contribution of analytical approaches is to provide a quick understanding of the critical structural and operational features determining the nature of competition in particular sectors and locations. These elements can then be isolated and become the subject of more extensive and rigorous examination and evaluation.

DICKSON, T. & BICKERSTAFFE, G. (EDS) (1999) *MASTERING GLOBAL BUSINESS,* F.T. PITMAN, LONDON

This work is produced as a joint venture between academics and researchers at Amos Tuck School, Dartmouth College, USA; HEC School of Management, Paris, France; IMD, Lausanne, Switzerland; and Templeton College, Oxford, UK. Ten areas are considered as follows.

» The environment in which business is becoming global.
» The need for global competitiveness.
» "Techno-world" – the relationship between technology and globalization.
» Creating global organizations.
» Controlling global organizations.
» Cross-cultural management and leadership.
» Serving global customers.
» Sourcing and managing global finance.
» Good citizenship: relations between business and governments.
» Regional perspectives.

Each is then written up from a variety of national, economic, social, political, and organizational behavior points of view. Each is supported with case examples from all over the world. The main lessons are the following.

» Global organizations require fully integrated and effective communication systems, supported and not driven by e-mail, websites, and virtual communications.
» Effective management across cultures and boundaries is only achieved through understanding and delivering advantages to all concerned, and this means attending to social, as well as operational, interests.

» Strategy and policy can never be effectively designed or implemented by headquarters in isolation from the locations of activities; nor can returns be controlled or predicted.

» Marketing is a global requirement and each individual location requires its own marketing strategy. While more general activities can be undertaken with the purpose of engaging general interest and awareness, the desire to purchase is only delivered when products and services are known, believed, and perceived to produce the distinctive benefits required by the specific customer or client group.

» The financial returns required must be capable of achievement. This requires the full understanding of the specific strength, depth, and duration of each market and location.

» Technology is neither universal, nor assured. Companies must be prepared to respond when specific operations are transformed as the result of invention or development elsewhere in the industry.

» Responsibility is a combination of compliance with laws and regulations; the social contribution that accrues from being a good employer or market provider and server; addressing specific issues such as waste and effluent, staff pay, and conditions of employment; and adopting responsible attitudes towards resource consumption and renewal.

Ten Steps for Effective Global Organization Management

This final chapter provides key insights into sustaining effective global organization management in today's business environment. It covers:

» strategic thinking;
» leadership;
» market and location understanding;
» investment, technology, and expertise command;
» merger and takeover;
» addition and subtraction;
» responsibility;
» management style;
» management development; and
» reinforcement.

INTRODUCTION

The capability to become, and remain, a truly global organization is based on the ability to command and deploy economic and other resources in order to assess particular markets and locations for opportunities. Based on the adoption of a generic strategic position, this means:

» global consideration, in which the decision is taken to be the premium provider in all sectors served;
» locally, in which global business is developed using a cost advantage, focus, or differentiated approach to each market;
» establishing, sustaining, and developing the desired presence in the particular markets. This requires strategic decisions on whether to seek to be the only or overwhelming player in markets (e.g. Microsoft); the largest single player (e.g. Coca-Cola in soft drinks); or fitting the presence to the precise locality (e.g. McDonald's is the main provider of fast food in the USA, a niche player only in Russia); and
» using the existing basis as the platform on which to base further growth, either through developing existing products and services into fresh areas, or looking for new opportunities potentially available as the result of physical presence or resources command.

Within this context, the following steps are required.

1. STRATEGIC THINKING

For global organizations, this means the ability to interrelate the following elements.

» *Thinking globally* – adopting a perspective that envisages the organization's products and services on sale in the axis economies and also remote locations (see summary box 10.1).

SUMMARY BOX 10.1: REMOTE LOCATIONS

One perceptual test of truly global thinking is the present knowledge base that exists among top managers and strategic analysts. For example, can the organization envisage working in: Anchorage, Alaska; Khartoum, Sudan; Dundee, Scotland; Tahiti, Western Pacific; or rural Brazil, Central Africa or Madagascar? However global the perceived approach may be, it has to be:

» on the one hand, capable of considering the whole world as having potential for activities and operations; and
» on the other hand, limited by where the priorities truly lie.

This has then to be re-evaluated in terms of distance, transport, logistics, and support so that activities are not conducted in corporate isolation however remote the physical location may be.
Source: University College London Working Paper (2001).

» *Thinking locally* – requiring investment in cultural, social, behavioral, and ethical understanding of the particular areas where business is envisaged. There may be strong religious customs or social norms, and patterns of work may be dictated by climate extremes. For example, a holiday resort building venture in Spain recently failed because the lead contractor, based in the UK, failed to recognize that building work could not, and did not, take place between the hours of 11.00 a.m. and 5.00 p.m. because the weather was too hot.
» *Thinking locality* – in terms of the nature of the business relationship that is to be developed and its basis in spending and consumption patterns; propensity to buy and consume local products and services; position and reputation of present providers; and forecast and projected investment levels and returns. This then needs developing into the basis of a *mutually* profitable relationship answering the questions:
  » what do we gain from them?
  » what do they gain from us?

The thinking mix required forms the basis on which particular opportunities and organizational resources are brought together. It also ensures that subjective elements of strategy and policy formulation are identified as such at an early stage for both good and bad reasons.

» *The good* – "We want to work in Montreal/St. Helena/Sakhalin because we are confident (very subjective) we can develop good business"; "We do not want to work in Colombo/London/Vancouver because we cannot quite see ourselves fitting in."

» *The bad* – "We want to work in Iceland/Chile/New Zealand because the market is just waiting for us to arrive" (arrogance); "We do not want to work in Ghana/Mexico/Australia because it is impossible to do business there" (reflecting social, and often, national or ethnic prejudice).

2. LEADERSHIP

Leadership that is truly global transcends prejudices and preconceptions, acknowledges the subjective elements, and matches and harmonizes these with the business drives and investment levels required.

Global leadership requires exceptional qualities.

» *Integrity* – as the basis for all corporate and managerial activities, and as the spine of organization culture and management style.

» *Humility* – recognizing that no corporation, however global, can possibly know and understand everything about all areas unless proper research and assessment is carried out; and recognizing that all organizations, managers and staff never stop learning and developing.

» *Enthusiasm* – the need for absolute commitment to all activities and locations; and where there are priorities, ensuring that everything is carried out with the same degree of personal, professional, and occupational enthusiasm, commitment, and energy whatever the position in the priority order.

» *Respect* – recognizing that staff activities and problems in remote locations require the same fundamental basis of value as those closer to headquarters. For example, the race and labor relations problems at Ford UK were compounded by the fact that for years nobody with real influence came from Detroit to see the situation for themselves. Respect must be earned. Those using powerful economic positions *can* gain entry, more or less, to the markets, sectors, and locations of their choice. Maintaining this presence means attending to the social and political elements, as well as market domination and exploitation. It is universally necessary to respect the fact that to those who live there, the Vietnamese (or Thai or French) "way" is as important as the American, UK, or German "way" as to those at headquarters.

Leaders must therefore be prepared to travel, visit, and understand, as well as act and accept advice and guidance from those on the ground in particular locations.

3. MARKET AND LOCATION UNDERSTANDING

Analyzing new and proposed areas and locations of activity is essential. The primary techniques for this are:

» Customer analyses (see Chapter 6).
» Porter's Five Forces and Competitor Analyses (see Chapter 9).

A broader approach is given by Cartwright (2001) which identifies a ten point approach under the acronym SPECTACLES as follows.

» *Social* - changes in society and societal trends; demographic trends and influences.
» *Political* - political processes and structures; lobbying; the political institutions of the locality, as well as global bodies such as the UN and NATO.
» *Economic* - referring especially to sources of finance; stock markets; inflation and interest rates; local, regional, national, and global economies.
» *Cultural* - international and national cultures; regional cultures; organization cultures; cultural clashes; cultural changes; cultural pressures on business and organizational activities.
» *Technological* - the relationship between technology, expertise, and work patterns; communications; virtual dimension; technology and production; and service activities.
» *Aesthetic* - communications; marketing and promotion; image; fashion; organizational body language; public relations.
» *Customer* - consumerism; the importance of analyzing customer bases; customer needs and wants; customer care; anticipating future customer requirements; customer behavior.

» *Legal* – sources of law; codes of practice; legal pressures; product and service liability; health and safety; national legislation.
» *Environmental* – responsibilities to the planet; pollution; waste management; environmental effects of specific activities; cost benefit analyses.
» *Sectoral* – competition; cartels and monopolies; competitive forces; cooperation within sectors; differentiation; and segmentation.

Building on the in-depth work required of the Porter approaches, Cartwright's model ensures that attention is paid to the "soft" elements of culture and aesthetics which are all too often neglected through sheer command of economic, expertise and technological power. Or else it is assumed that because things are socially and aesthetically acceptable and pleasing to the global organization's country of origin, they will be so, or can be imposed, on all locations.

4. INVESTMENT, TECHNOLOGY, AND EXPERTISE COMMAND

Global organizations are more or less certain to have, or to be able to call upon, these resources when required. The key issues are how to use them and how to develop them.

Usage

Investment appraisal requires a behavioral and managerial perspective, as well as drives for financial returns on investment. Ventures fail, or fall short of full success, because analyses and forecasts about what might happen in the future gain a life of their own and come to be read and understood as statements of fact rather than projection. Assumptions (which require testing) become preconceptions. These, in turn, are fuelled by sheer corporate size (and often vanity and arrogance). Perceptions of assured success become a matter of record before a single activity has been undertaken.

Development

Maximizing and optimizing long-term investment and returns depends on commitment to the establishment of an enduring presence in the location. From this is developed a range of corporate, collective, and individual relationships with potential suppliers, customers, and clients, and also politicians, lobbies, and vested interests. The need is to understand how everyone thinks, behaves, and acts, as well as commercial expectations and demands.

Once activities are commenced, customer, client, and supplier liaison is then engaged from the same point of view as on more familiar ground, with recognition of the prevailing cultural, social, and commercial customs and norms. This is also likely to be a much more successful and comfortable general approach, especially if the particular sector or location has had bad experiences with MNCs in the past.

5. MERGER AND TAKEOVER

The merger and takeover route to a global presence is attractive because it is quick. Going concerns can be bought up so that the economic size of the global organization and local reputation of the acquired company strengthen each other for the new range of activities.

Problems in the area are endemic however. About 90 per cent of mergers and takeovers fail. This is overwhelmingly because there is insufficient attention to cultural fit. Organizations look right for each other on paper. Overt mutual interests are easily identified. However, in terms of management style, collective attitudes and values, and the application of technology and expertise, there is no coincidence of interest or value. Problems are normally compounded, rather than addressed effectively, because the global organization then uses its economic might to remove the local partner's prevailing culture and key figures rather than addressing its own shortcomings.

Nor is this confined to takeover of local partners in new locations (see summary box 10.2).

SUMMARY BOX 10.2: THE MERGER OF SMITHKLINEBEECHAM AND GLAXO-WELLCOME

The first proposed merger of SmithKlineBeecham and Glaxo-Wellcome foundered because the members of the two companies' executive boards could not agree on who would do what job in the new merged organization. The proposal consequently took an additional three years to come to fruition.

When it was finally achieved in 1999, the new company emerged as SmithKlineGlaxo. This company is now the third largest in the world.

It has however, had substantial problems reducing headcount and property costs in non-productive areas. "Synergies and economies of scale" have become extremely expensive to achieve. Preconceptions of technological dominance took no account of the fit of technology and expertise when the two companies were brought together. The company has also had more general labor relations problems concerning the "rightsizing" of all operations, especially research and development, and headquarters restructuring.

6. ADDITION AND SUBTRACTION

Organizations entering new markets and locations must know what they expect to achieve, why and how, and what the market expects from them and why.

If circumstances change for any reason, the whole approach requires reappraisal. These circumstances may be within the organization's control or not (see summary box 10.3).

SUMMARY BOX 10.3: MATTERS OUTSIDE THE CONTROL OF GLOBAL ORGANIZATIONS

Examples

» Consumer goods: fashion and taste can never be imposed on any market. Regardless of location, marketing and advertising campaigns have to be engaged in order to persuade people to buy the perceived benefits. In the particular example of clothing, people will stop buying branded garments if the perception and reality of sweatshop manufacture ever outweighs the marketing of consumer benefits.

» Capital goods: for example, defense and electronic companies producing equipment for the Cold War have had to turn to other

> markets and activities. This has not always been easily achieved, and has led to extensive job losses at Dassault (France) and Plessey Marconi (UK) from 1994 to the present.
> » University education: UK universities funded budget shortfalls in the period 1991–97 through attracting full fee students from South East Asia. When the Asian currencies then collapsed, the universities had nothing further on which to fall back.

It is also essential to realize that market evaluation activities are universal. If one company has seen potential in an area, others will also have done so. The potential for competition therefore always exists.

Where global organizations are able to drive others out of particular sectors, they drive out all of the goodwill and mutual value that existed between suppliers, customers, clients, and the previous players. This has to be replaced with positive benefits on the part of the incomer. There is no basis for sustained effective and profitable activities if a void is created.

7. RESPONSIBILITY

Specific global organization responsibilities extend to present *and future* generations of:

» backers, financiers, and stockholders: in terms of returns on investments, returns on capital employed, dividends, and enhanced values;
» customers and clients: as the ultimate beneficiaries of the products and services; and who, in turn, provide the financial returns required for the present and future;
» staff: to provide all that is necessary for a long-term secure and productive relationship. Where this is not envisaged, staff always understand this. While it may be possible to gain their compliance, it will not secure their loyalty; and
» suppliers: supply side management effectiveness has suffered in the past from (superficial) management wisdom as follows:
  » multiple sourcing is a "good thing" because it keeps suppliers on their toes;

 » always buy from the cheapest source to keep costs down;
 » never pay on time;
 » it is possible to switch most suppliers at short notice, if not instantly.

Global organizations *can* do any one of these because of their sheer financial size. This stores up substantial problems for all. The global organization gains a reputation for being bad for business on the supply side. This then quickly translates into a wider loss of reputation. Suppliers are unable to plan their own operations with any degree of certainty. They may become dependent for existence on the global organization (and then have their own prices driven down). They find themselves unable to keep the rest of their client base satisfied, and so they begin to lose reputation.

8. MANAGEMENT STYLE

The need is to balance integrity and openness with market, social, and cultural expectations. Any organization that takes advantage of its dominant position to oppress staff, suppliers, customers, and clients is only able to sustain this until competition exists (see summary box 10.4).

SUMMARY BOX 10.4: VIRGIN AND BUSINESS PROPOSALS

The Virgin Group is headed by Richard Branson and based in the UK. It has expanded from music production and distribution into air and rail travel, financial services, publishing, computer games, property management, bridal wear, and film production.

Initial business evaluation is conducted on a combination of strong corporate culture and rigorous sector appraisal as follows.

 » The new venture must be in an existing well-understood sector.
 » The new venture must be capable of "Virgin presentation" and a sense of fun that is deemed to go with this.
 » The sector is under-developed for some reason.

> » The sector is ethical – the company does not engage in tobacco or armaments production.
> » The customers and/or suppliers are being ill-served or oppressed by the existing players.
>
> This the company sees as being an opportunity for others to exploit. This is because, given the choice, suppliers, customers, and clients prefer to do business with those who adopt a more overtly wholesome approach.

Management style is established at headquarters where overarching standards are set. These are then delivered at regional and local levels according to the following.

» Cultural demands (see Hofstede, Chapter 8): for example, it is ineffective to engage in participative local management if the staff involved do not understand what is expected of them. Prescriptive (or any other) management style requires fundamental integrity and an approach with which the staff are comfortable.
» Management structures: it is usual to establish patterns of regional and local managers (ABB call these "local chieftains" – see Chapter 7) who carry devolved authority, responsibility and accountability. They set operational standards for their areas in accordance with overall strategy, policy, and direction (see summary box 10.5).

SUMMARY BOX 10.5: OVER-MIGHTY SUBJECTS

In sixteenth century England the Tudor kings and queens were burdened with what came to be known as their over-mighty subjects. These were the land-owning nobility whose support the monarch required to keep the peace in outlying parts of the country and who, if support was not forthcoming, constituted a real threat to the monarch's position. Support was therefore generated by giving financial rewards, local ruling rights, and general autonomy to these nobles in return for their continued allegiance to the dynasty. Great areas of the country therefore effectively became the personal kingdoms of these nobles.

In global organizations, over-mighty subjects are found in areas equivalent, especially regional and local offices in remote locations away from headquarters.

9. MANAGEMENT DEVELOPMENT

All management development is based on the ability to acquire and apply the required behavior, attitudes, skills, knowledge, expertise, and technological proficiency.

Global managers require continuous development in:

» macro economic, social and political pressures, swings and influences;
» cultural, social and behavioral awareness in relation to the specific locations in which they are to work, and in which the organization has interests;
» technological and expertise availability, application, and usage in particular locations; and organization of work, supply, and distribution patterns according to the specific pressures and constraints present;
» decision-making and executive expertise in the context in which it is to be applied;
» specific patterns of communication, reinforcement, visibility, and access; and
» problem-solving capability in the context in which these arise.

There is a more or less universal requirement for all this to be supported by high levels of education and professional development. This must then be developed through cultural, social, and location-based learning. Specific skills such as languages, technological and operational understanding are also required; and these must be supported through the availability of interpreters and technicians. Effective global management development is based on the premises that securing long-term profitable and effective presence means harmonizing organizational objectives with local habits, and that a basis of partnership is required between the organization and its suppliers, staff, customers, clients, and community.

10. REINFORCEMENT

Global organization presence is never an end in itself. Markets have to be developed. New products and services must be made available, together with quality of delivery and support. The staff are entitled to enhanced and improved pay and conditions of employment.

Problems are certain to occur where the relationship is known and believed to be purely exploitative. For example, manufacturing companies in the garment industry fully understand that they are only as secure as their present order book; crews on "flags of convenience" cruise ships know that a good performance on the current voyage is no guarantee of re-engagement.

These positions are only sustainable until those in the dependent position develop themselves to the point at which they are able to operate with sufficient degrees of autonomy and independence. In the short to medium-term in many cases, this is not a burning issue for the global organization. In the longer-term, political, social and economic changes, and enhanced capability in what is presently the third world, are all going to bring pressures for a much more responsible approach from global organizations.

CONCLUSIONS

The main conclusions are:

» being a global organization is a function of resource, technology, and expertise command made possible by the ability to put high enduring and sustainable levels of capital into chosen ventures;
» global organizations require the capability to "play away" – to carry out their activities in local and regional ways; and
» the managers of global organizations have a range of moral, social, and ethical responsibilities in addition to financial demands.

Because of the transition from political to corporate power, managers are placed in the position previously held by politicians and public servants – attending to social demands and requirements. The need to sustain enduring profit levels is well understood in all corporate circles. Managing the social aspects, the key to ensuring stability, is not fully realized. It must be developed if positive conditions for globalized activities are to be maintained and enhanced.

BIBLIOGRAPHY AND FURTHER READING

Cartwright, R. (2000) *Mastering Customer Relations*, Macmillan Palgrave, Basingstoke.

Drucker, P.F. (2000) *Management Challenges for the 21st Century*, Harper Business, London.

Gates, B. (1998) *Business @ the Speed of Thought*, Penguin, London.

Gratton, L. (2000) *Living Strategy: Putting People at the Heart of Corporate Purpose*, F.T. Prentice Hall, New Jersey.

Heller, R. (1998) *In Search of European Excellence*, Harper Collins Business, London.

Hamel, G. and Prahalad, C.K. (1998) *Competing for the Future*, Harvard Business School Press, Boston.

Liebowitz, S.J. and Margolis, S.E. (1992) *Winners, Losers and Microsoft*, Independent Institute, New York.

Maund, L. (2000) *An Introduction to Human Resource Management*, Macmillan Palgrave, Basingstoke.

Morita, A. (1992) *Made in Japan: The Sony Story*, Fontana, London.

Pettinger, R. (1998) *Managing the Flexible Workforce*, Cassell, London.

Pettinger, R. (2000) *Investment Appraisal: A Managerial Approach*, Macmillan Palgrave, Basingstoke.

Pettinger, R. (2001) *Mastering Management Skills*, Macmillan Palgrave, Basingstoke.

Senge, P. (1992) *The Fifth Discipline*, Century Business, New York.

Sternberg, E. (1997) *Just Business: Business Ethics in Action*, Warner, New York.

Sutton, C. (1999) *Strategic Concepts*, Macmillan Palgrave, Basingstoke.

Pascale, R. and Athos, A. (1992) *The Art of Japanese Management*, Fontana, London.

Rice, J. (1998) *Doing Business in Japan*, Penguin, London.

Wheeler, D. and Sillanpaa, M. (1997) *The Stakeholder Corporation*, Pitman Publishing, London.

Frequently Asked Questions (FAQs)

Q1: What are global organizations?

A: See Chapters 2, 3 and 7.

Q2: What is globalization?

A: See Chapters 1, 2, 3, 7 and 9.

Q3: Why is globalization contentious?

A: See Chapters 1, 2, 3, 7 and 9.

Q4: What do global organizations do that others do not?

A: See Chapters 1, 2, 3, 7 and 9.

Q5: What are the strengths of global organizations?

A: See Chapters 1, 2, 3, 7 and 9.

Q6: What are their responsibilities? How should they discharge these?

A: See Chapters 1, 2, 3, 7 and 9.

Q7: What are "global managers?"

A: See Chapters 1, 2, 3, 7 and 9

Q8: What are the alternatives to global organizations and global managers?

A: See Chapters 1, 2, 3, 7 and 9

Q9: Why do some organizations go global and others not?

A: See Chapters 3, 4, 5, 6 and 10.

Q10: What does the future hold – for global organizations and those that wish to become so?

A: See Chapters 4, ,5 ,6, 7, 9 and 10.

Index

Printed and bound by CPI Group (UK) Ltd, Croydon, CR0 4YY

13/04/2025

14656560-0005